Your Solar Home

The Art & Science of Heating, Cooling & Powering Your Home with the Sun

Guidebook

Your Solar Home – Guidebook
"The Art and Science of Heating, Cooling, and Powering Your Home with the Sun"

A Rahus Institute –Solar Schoolhouse Publication

Written and illustrated by Clay Atchison
Projects designed by Tor Allen, Hal Aronson, and Clay Atchison
Historical sections and images provided by John Perlin

For more information write:

The Rahus Institute
1535 Center Ave.
Martinez, CA 94553 USA
925-370-7262
www.rahus.org
www.solarschoolhouse.org

Cover Design by Anne Washmera, www.amcdesigns.net
Solar Home model is based on the Missouri-Rolla Solar Home entry in the 2005 Solar Decathlon competition in Washington DC. Solar roof includes solar electrical and thermal hydrid design. Photo by Tor Allen.

Printed by Alonzo Printing, Hayward, California, on 100% recycled paper with 100% post-consumer waste content (New Leaf).

ISBN-10 0-9776342-0-5
ISBN-13 978-0-9776342-0-0

1. Solar Energy   2. Environment   3. Education
First Edition

Contents

Acknowledgements...vi
Introduction...vii

Chapter 1: Facing the Sun

How to Get More Solar Energy All Year Long 12
Earth's Poles, The Equator, Northern & Southern Hemispheres, Day & Night
The Reasons for the Seasons 13
The Earth's axis is tilted, Earth's Orbit, Solstices & Equinoxes
Why Is It Colder In Winter?... 14
The Sun's Arc, Energy & Sun Angles
There are Two North Poles 15
True North & Magnetic North, Magnetic Declination Maps

Chapter 2: Understanding Heat

What Happens When an Object Gets Hot?............................. 20
Heat is a form of energy: the energy of atoms in motion, Atoms & Molecules
Hot Objects Expand
Radiation, Convection & Conduction 21
Light & Heat, Radiation & Heat Transfer, Colors & Heat, Conduction in Solids,
Convection in Liquids, Air Acts Like a Liquid
Insulation Blocks Heat Flow 24
Stationary Air Acts as an Insulator 25

Chapter 3: Solar Ovens

How to Cook Food With The Sun.. 30
The Greenhouse Effect, A Solar Box Cooker
Principles of Solar Cooking 31
Bring in Sunlight, Absorb the Heat, Keep the Heat
Solar History: Solar Cooking 32

Chapter 4: Solar Hot Water

Heating Water With Sunlight 36
Standard Water Heaters, Solar Batch Heaters
Solar Collectors 37
Solar for Swimming Pools, Flat Plate Collectors
Using Solar Collectors 38
Thermosiphon Systems, Drainback Systems
Tankless Water Heaters 40
Heat Exchangers, Solar Preheat
Solar History: Solar Water Heating 41

Chapter 5: Passive Solar Design

How to Stay Comfortable All Year Long 48
House Location & Position 48
Seasonal Shading, Wind Blocks, Trees & Hills
South Facing Windows 49
Windows & Heat Loss
Insulation & Thermal Mass 50
Direct Gain Systems, Sunspaces, Trombe Walls, Day & Night Heating
Convection Currents & Cooling 53
Nighttime cooling, Daytime cooling, Earth cooling
Daylighting 54
Overhangs, Curtains & Blinds, Skylights, Shading, Clerestories
Solar History: Solar Design 57

Chapter 6: Solar Electricity

Making Electricity with Photovoltaics 64
Photons, Electrons, Protons, Electrical Charges
The Photovoltaic Effect 65
Solar cells, Modules & Arrays, Sun Angles, Tilt Angles, Shadows
Basic Electrical Circuits 68
Elements of electrical circuits, Volts, Amps, Watts
Increasing Power 70
Series & Parallel Wiring, The Power Formula
Using Solar Electricity 72
PV direct systems, Battery backup systems, DC & AC, Inverters, Utility Intertie
Solar History: Photovoltaics 75

Chapter 7: System Sizing

How Much Energy Do You Need? **84**
Using Energy Efficiently, Energy Guide Label, Phantom Loads & Vampires
Energy Audits **88**
Measuring Electricity Use, Rate of Energy Use, Watts & Kilowatts,
Total Energy Used, Watt-Hours and Kilowatt Hours
Auditing Loads **90**
Hours of Use, Electric Bills
Electric meters **92**
Array sizing **94**
Peak Sun, Peak Sun Hours, Peak Sun Hours per Day, Module Output,
System Sizing Worksheet **96**

Projects.. **99**

Glossary **123**

Index.. **127**

Acknowledgements

Thanks goes to the following organizations for supporting various experiences and development of solar educational materials, the sum of which is this book and video: California Energy Commission, Alameda Power & Telecom, Berkeley Ecohouse, Rising Sun Energy Center, City of Palo Alto Utilities, City of Lodi Electric Utility Department, Imperial Irrigation District, San Diego Regional Energy Office, US DOE Million Solar Roofs, Sacramento Municipal Utility District, Roseville Electric, Association for Environmental Outdoor Educators, Pasadena Water & Power, Redwood Energy Authority, Anaheim Public Utilities, SMA-America, Home Power, Imperial Valley Regional Occupational Program, Solar Living Institute, and Solar Energy International.

Special thanks to Imperial Irrigation District and the City of Lodi Electric Utility for financial support with composing the Guidebook.

Thanks to the many schools and teachers working to integrate solar energy into their classrooms, with a special thanks to:
Carolyn Griffith (Alameda High School – Alameda, CA)
Leslie Dumas (San Ramon Valley High School – Danville, CA)
Otak Jump (Ohlone Elementary School – Palo Alto, CA)
Lisa Wu (Gunn High School - Palo Alto, CA)
Jim Jones (Valley View Elementary School - Coachella, CA)
Andrea Hardman (Pioneer Elementary School – Brentwood, CA)
Robert Macholtz (Central Union High School - El Centro, CA)
Bill Dodge (Lincoln Middle School – Alameda, CA)
Lise Schikel Goddard (Midlands School – Los Olivos, CA)
Chris Dolan (Wilson Middle School – Indio, CA)
Kerry Langdale (Canyon High School – Anaheim, CA)
Maureen Kleppe (Weimar Hills School – Weimar, CA)
Randy Smith (Brawley High School – Brawley, CA)
Nancy Kellogg (Brawley High School – Brawley, CA)
Wilton Goo (Calipatria High School – Calipatria, CA)
Michael Gohl (The SunWorks – Niland, CA)
Jeff Campbell (Indio High School – Indio, CA)
Kathy Swartz (Camp Arroyo Outdoor School – Livermore, CA)
Eric Schlavin (Sierra Ridge Middle School – Pollock Pines, CA)
Maurie Jacinto (Victor Elementary School – Victor, CA)
Keith Jacinto (Reese Elementary School, Lodi, CA)
Dave Greulich (Lodi High School – Lodi, CA)
Roger Crane (Bear Creek High School – Stockton, CA)
Joel Hadsall (Bear Creek High School – Stockton, CA)
Brenda Huiras (Elkhorn Elementary School – Stockton, CA)
Julie Chinnock (Lodi SDA Elementary – Lodi, CA)
Susan Massey (Holtville High School, Holtville, CA)
Eduardo Neibla (Holtville High School, Holtville, CA)
Alfonso Massey (in Memory of – Imperial, CA)
David Avila (Holtville Middle & High Schools, Holtville, CA)

Thanks to reviewers: Eric Schlavin, Maureen Kleppe, Otak Jump, Andrea Hardman, Jim Jones, Dena Allen, Jannike Allen, Pauline Allen, and Joe Armstrong.

Introduction

Your Solar Home

This book shows you how to use solar energy in your home.

You'll see how to keep your house warm in the winter, and cool in the summer, using just sunlight for fuel.

Not only that, you will find out how to heat water and cook food with the Sun. You'll even see how to turn sunlight into electricity.

Usually we do these things by burning fossil fuels like coal and natural gas. But fossil fuels are running out, and burning them is hurting the environment.

The Sun, however, is a non-polluting source of energy that should last for billions of years.

This book starts by explaining what solar energy is, and how to get as much of it as we need throughout the year.

We then find out how sunlight is transformed into heat, and how this heat can be transferred and stored. Several ways to use the Sun's heat are presented.

Next the book shows how to make electricity from sunlight, and how to use that electricity in many different ways.

There are also sections on the way earlier societies used solar power, from the early Greeks to modern America.

Solar Powered Projects

To understand how to use solar energy, you can build things that use sunlight as fuel. The first projects are very simple, and use everyday materials.

There are also more advanced projects, like solar race cars, that use special equipment. Information on where to obtain the special equipment can be found at the Solar Schoolhouse website: *www.solarschoolhouse.org*

Solar Powered Projects

Boxes like this appear throughout the book. They show projects you can make that use solar power. For complete details go to the projects section at the back of the book.

Pizza Box Solar Oven
This oven can bake brownies with the sun.

Review Questions and Further Exploration

The end of each chapter has review questions to increase your understanding of solar power. If you have further questions, or would like to explore solar energy in more detail, go to the Solar Schoolhouse website: *www.solarschoolhouse.org*

Now let's begin exploring Your Solar Home.

1 **Facing the Sun**

How to Get More Solar Energy All Year Long

You get the most solar energy when facing the sun directly. In the United States you turn toward the south pole to face the sun. To see why this is so, let's look at the Earth in space.

A compass "needle" is a magnet that points toward the Earth's poles.

The Earth is a giant ball spinning on it's north-south axis. This axis is an imaginary line through the center of the Earth from the north pole to the south pole.

Around the middle of the Earth is another imaginary line called the **equator**.

The equator divides the planet into two halves called **hemispheres**.

The United States in is in the northern hemisphere, the half of the Earth on the north pole side of the equator.

At noon, a person standing on the equator would see the Sun directly overhead.

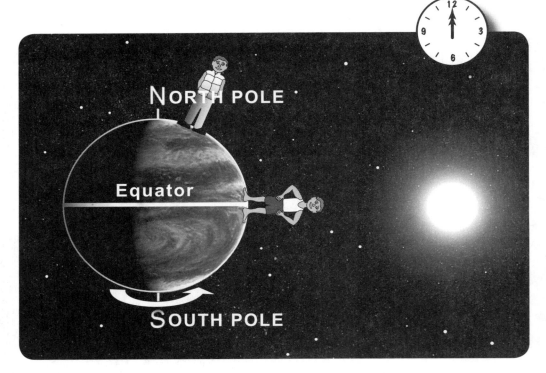

The closer you are to the north pole, the farther south the Sun is in the sky.

A person standing closer to the north pole would see the Sun at an angle. To the second person, the Sun would be lower in the southern sky, closer to the equator. This is the reason you look toward the south to face the Sun in the northern hemisphere.

Day & Night

The Earth spins around once on its axis every 24 hours. When our part of the Earth is facing the Sun, it's day. When we're facing away, it's night.

Because the Earth is spinning, we see the sun move across the sky during the day. The Sun rises in the east and sets in the west.

The Reasons for the Seasons

What causes the seasons? Some people think it's because the Earth is closer to the Sun in the summer, and farther away in the winter. That seems like it might be true, but actually the Earth is 3 million miles closer to the sun in January than it is in July. Besides, when it's summer in the northern hemisphere, it's winter in the southern hemisphere.

To find out why we have winter, spring, summer and fall, we need to know one more very important thing about the Earth's north-south axis:

The Earth's axis is tilted

The Earth's poles are not straight up and down. The north-south axis is tilted 23.5 degrees. This tilt causes the changes in the seasons.

Remember the Earth isn't just spinning on it's axis; it's also traveling around the Sun. Every year the Earth orbits the Sun in a huge circle through space.

During summer in the northern hemisphere (June to September), the north pole is tilted toward the sun. This causes the northern half of the Earth to receive more light and heat than it does during winter (December to March). On June 21st, the first day of summer, the northern hemisphere is tilted the most toward the Sun. This is called the **Summer Solstice**, and it's the longest day of the year.

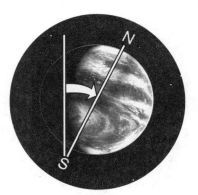

Earth's axis is tilted 23.5 degrees.

As the Earth continues its orbit, it passes a point where its tilt is sideways to the Sun. This is called the **Autumnal Equinox**. Both day and night are the same length.

The Earth reaches the other side of the Sun on the shortest day of the year, the **Winter Solstice.** This is the first day of winter, and the northern hemisphere is tilted farthest away from the Sun.

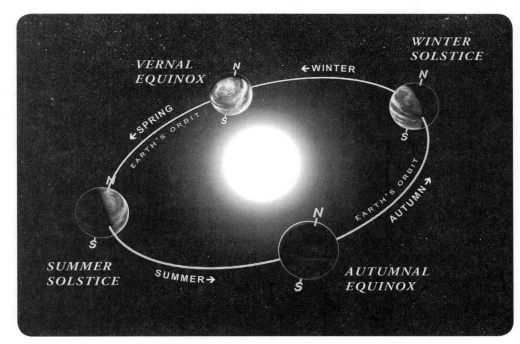

The tilt of the Earth's axis causes the seasons.

As the Earth travels back toward summer it passes another point where the axis is tilted sideways to the Sun. Once again day and night are the same length. This day is called the **Vernal Equinox**.

Why Is It Colder In Winter?

Light is strongest when it hits an object straight on. This happens near the **equator**, the invisible line around the middle of the Earth. At the equator the weather is warm all year long.

Closer to the poles the energy from the sun is spread out and, therefore, not as strong. The north pole is constantly frozen because the sunlight is so spread out and weak. (See graphics on page 22)

During summer in the northen hemisphere, the north pole tilts toward the sun, and sunlight hits the top half of the Earth more directly. During winter, the north pole tilts away and the energy from the sun is weaker.

Summer

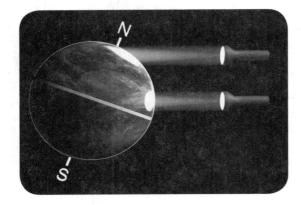

In summer the pole tilts toward the Sun.

The sun's heat is strong at the equator all year long.

Winter

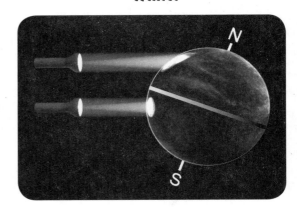

In winter the pole tilts away.

Seen from the Earth's surface, the sun's path across the sky changes during the year. The sun's arc from east to west is lower in the sky during the winter.

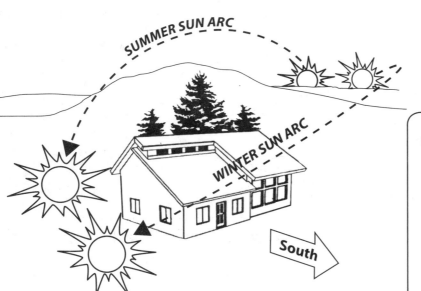

The sun arc is lower in the southern sky in the winter.

At noon in the middle of summer, the sun is almost directly overhead. At noon in the middle of winter, the sun is lower in the sky towards the south.

Project #1   Cereal Box Sundial

Learn how to use a shadow to tell the time of day.

There are Two North Poles

You might be surprised to know that a magnetic compass does not usually point to the true north pole. The compass needle actually points to a different place called the **magnetic north pole**. The magnetic north pole is in northern Canada.

Not only that, the magnetic north pole is moving! It's traveling in a northwesterly direction at about **26 miles per year**. The magnetic pole also wanders daily around an average position.

The angle between the magnetic north pole and the true north pole is called **magnetic declination**.

This angle changes over the course of many years.

The angle between magnetic north and true north also depends on where you are on the Earth's surface.

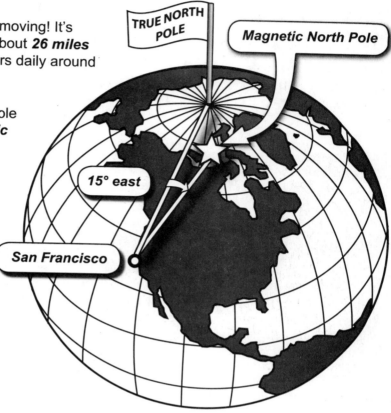

Viewed from San Francisco, the magnetic north pole is about 15° to the east of the true north pole.

East Declination

Suppose you were in San Francisco, and wanted to find the true north pole with a compass.

If you pointed the "N" of the compass toward the true north pole, the **compass needle** would point 15 degrees to the right (or east) of north.

We say that the magnetic declination in San Francisco is 15 degrees east.

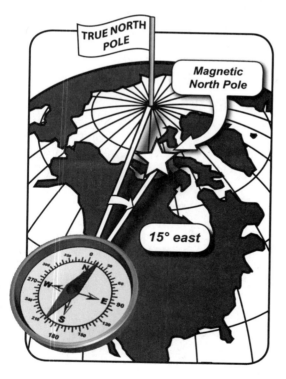

In San Francisco a compass needle reads 15° east when the "N" (north cardinal point) points true north.

West Declination

Viewed from Boston, magnetic north is about 15 degrees to the left or **west** of true north. This is west declination of 15 degrees.

In Boston, a compass needle points 15 degrees west of north when the "N" points toward the true north pole.

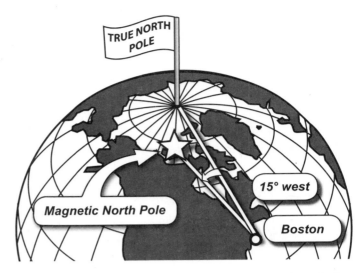

Viewed from Boston, the magnetic north pole is about 15° to the right of the true north pole.

Magnetic Declination Maps

In order to find true north or south from any location, you can use Magnetic Declination Maps. *Remember: the magnetic north pole moves in a northwesterly direction about 26 miles per year!* To get the most current maps visit websites such as the National Geophysical Data Center at:

http://www.ngdc.noaa.gov

NOTE: A web link to the National Geophsical Data Center is also available at the Solar Schoolhouse website: **www.solarschoolhouse.org**

United States Magnetic Declination 2004

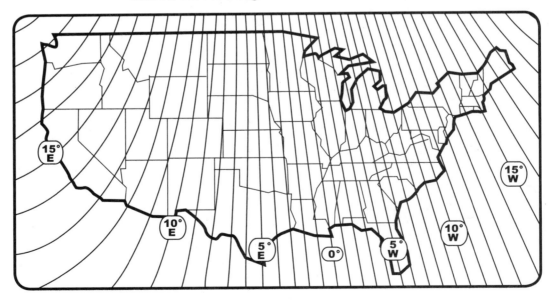

This map shows what your compass needle will read when the "N" (north cardinal point) points toward the true north pole.

Review Questions

1. An imaginary line called the _____ divides the Earth into two halves called _____.

2. The Earth's north-south axis is tilted:
   A. To the south
   B. Toward the solstices
   C. 23.5 degrees

3. At noon in the summer, a person at the equator would see the sun overhead. At the same time, a person closer to the north pole would always see the sun:
   A. Lower in the southern sky
   B. At an easterly angle
   C. Over their right shoulder

3. It's colder in the winter because the Earth is:
   A. Farther from the Sun
   B. Tilted on its axis
   C. Covered with clouds
   D. All of the above

4. Because the Earth is spinning on its axis, the Sun moves across the sky from _____ to _____.

5. _____ is the season when the Sun's path is lowest in the sky.

6. When is the northern hemisphere tilted most toward the Sun?
   A. July 24
   B. The Vernal Equinox
   C. The Summer Sosltice

7. A compass needle points toward the _____.

8. True or False (Circle one): The Earth's magnetic north pole is moving.

9. _____ is the angle between true north and magnetic north.

10. When the "N" on a compass is pointing toward true north, the compass needle will show:
   A. The magnetic declination
   B. True south
   C. The distance from the equator
   D. None of the above

2 Understanding Heat

What Happens When an Object Gets Hot?

To heat our homes with sunlight, we first need to understand what heat is, and how heat flows from one object to another.

Heat is a form of energy: the energy of atoms in motion

All matter is made of incredibly tiny particles called atoms. Atoms are usually clustered together in groups called molecules. Atoms and molecules are constantly moving and jiggling. The hotter an object is, the faster its molecules vibrate. The faster they vibrate, the more space they take up.

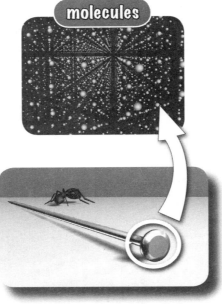

Everything is made of vibrating atoms.

Atoms are often found in groups called molecules.

Molecules are so small that there are trillions & trillions of them in the head of a pin.

The hotter an object is, the faster its molecules vibrate.

Hot Objects Expand

As a substance heats up, its tiny particles vibrate faster, and push each other farther apart. This makes the substance expand and become lighter.

That is why a hot air balloon floats. The hotter air inside takes up more space, and is lighter than the outside air.

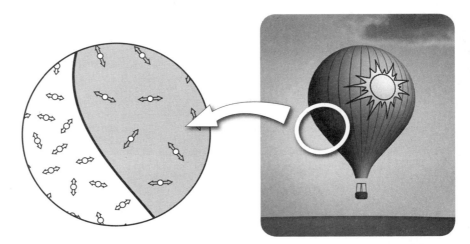

Hotter air inside the balloon is lighter than the cool air outside.

Radiation, Convection & Conduction

Heat always flows from warmer areas to cooler areas. It only stops flowing when both areas reach the same temperature.

This heat energy moves from hotter places to cooler places in three ways: through **radiation, convection and conduction.**

The liquid in this thermometer expands when heated.

RADIATION *is the direct transfer of heat by electromagnetic waves*

Light behaves in two different ways. It acts both like waves, and like particles. When sunlight behaves like waves we call them **electromagnetic waves**.

When sulight acts like particles we call these individual packets of energy **photons**.

Electromagnetic waves can move through the vacuum of space, and can also move through air or water.

The sun produces different kinds of light.

These include: visible light, ultraviolet light, and infrared light, as well as several other types of energy.

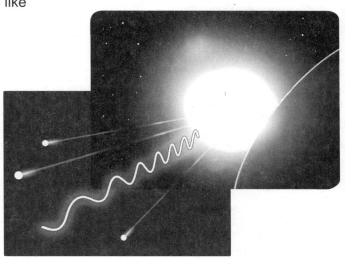

Sunlight acts both like waves and like particles.

Infrared light is also called heat (or heat waves)

All light causes things to heat up, but infrared light causes the biggest temperature rise. Most of the energy that reaches us from the sun is infrared radiation and visible light. When an object warms up, it gives off heat as infrared radiation too.

Dark Colors absorb more heat.

When sunlight strikes an object it's either absorbed into the object or bounces off, depending upon how reflective the surface is.

Black surfaces absorb almost all of the sunlight that falls on them.

White and mirror-like surfaces reflect light and heat.

Black surfaces absorb heat.

White surfaces reflect heat.

More energy is absorbed per unit of area when light falls at a 90 degree angle

The amount of heat absorbed by an object also depends upon the angle at which the heat waves strike it.

The greatest amount of heat is absorbed when light strikes straight on at a 90 degree angle.

more heat per square inch   *less heat per square inch*

If the angle is more slanted, the same amount of light covers a bigger area. Less heat is absorbed for each unit of area.

Once absorbed, sunlight turns into heat.

Much of the energy from sunlight comes as visible light.

This energy is converted into heat once sunlight is absorbed into an object.

Sunlight is absorbed into the black surface, and changes into heat.

The hot suface then radiates heat.

The hotter it becomes, the more an object gives off heat waves.

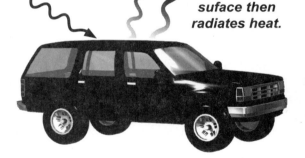

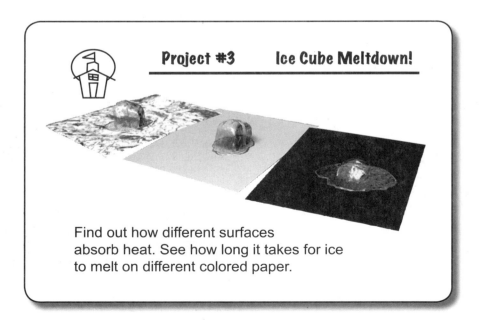

Project #3   Ice Cube Meltdown!

Find out how different surfaces absorb heat. See how long it takes for ice to melt on different colored paper.

CONDUCTION *is the movement of heat through a solid substance*

When one end of a metal bar is held in a flame, the other end gets hot too. The heat is moving through the bar by **conduction**.

Let's see what's happening at the atomic level:

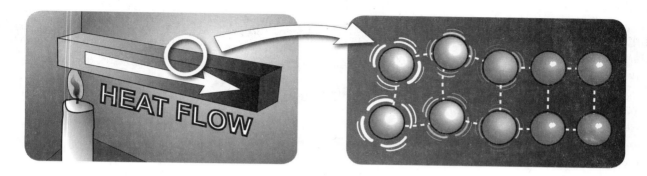

Each metal atom is attached to its neighbors. As the atoms heat up, they jiggle faster, and cause the neighboring atoms to shake too. Soon the energy spreads through the entire bar.

Because the atoms are so tiny we can't see them jiggling, but we can feel the temperature increasing at the other end of the metal bar.

Substances that transfer heat well are callled **conductors**. Metals, especially copper and aluminum, transfer heat easily, and are good conductors.

CONVECTION *is the movement of heat through liquids*

Heat can travel through liquids and gases as moving currents. If water isn't moving, it's a poor conductor, and heat moves through it slowly. But if currents start moving in water, they transfer heat more quickly. This is the process of heat transfer by **convection**.

Remember: when gases or liquids are heated, the area closest to the heat source expands and rises.

This is what happens to a pot of water on a stovetop. As water close to the burner heats up, it rises. The colder water at the sides moves into the space left by the rising hot water. This kind of movement in liquids is called a **convection current**.

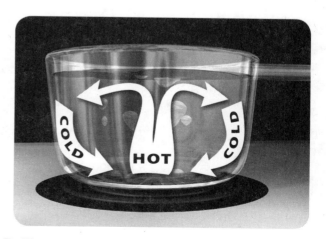

Boiling water in a pot forms convection currents.

Convection Currents transfer heat through air too

Even though air isn't wet, it transfers heat the same way liquids do: by convection. If it's standing still, air is a very poor conductor, and transfers heat very slowly. But if air currents start flowing, they transfer heat very well.

Look at the example to the right. Because the road pavement is black, it absorbs more radiation from the sun, and heats up. The air directly above the hot road heats up too, and starts to rise.

The lighter colored fields next to the road reflect more of the sun's heat, and stay cooler. The cooler air above the fields moves into the space left by the rising hot air, and convection currents form.

Convection currents transfer heat through the air.

Insulation blocks heat flow

Now we know how heat flows from one object to another. Remember, heat will continue to flow from the hotter object to the cooler object until both are the same temperature. But sometimes we want to keep objects at different temperatures.

On a cold day we probably want to keep our bodies warmer by wearing thick clothes. When camping, we use thick sleeping bags to stay warm through the cold night. In both cases we're using insulation to slow the movement of heat from our bodies to the cold outside air.

Insulation is a substance that slows down convection and conduction.

Many materials, such as styrofoam and leather, are poor conductors and transfer heat slowly. Poor conductors are also called **insulators**.

Reflective materials can stop heat from flowing by radiation. But how do we slow down heat transfer by convection?

Remember that if air is standing still, it transfers heat very slowly. If we can trap the air, and keep it from moving, convection currents won't be able to form.

This sleeping bag is filled with goose down, an excellent insulator.

Stationary air acts as an insulator

Let's look inside a down vest. The down stuffing has thousands of tiny spaces that trap air, and keep currents from flowing. This trapped air now acts as an insulator.

The thicker the layer of trapped air, the harder it is for the heat to escape.

Down stuffing has thousands of air spaces to trap heat.

Now that we know what heat is, and how heat moves from one place to another, we can use this information to do many useful things. In the next chapter we'll see how to use this knowledge to cook food with sunlight.

Project #4   Save That Ice Cube!

See how insulation can keep an ice cube from melting. Have a contest to see who can keep their ice cube frozen the longest..

Review Questions

1. Heat is a form of _____.

2. When a substance heats up, it:
A. Expands
B. Shrinks
C. Rotates

3. The hotter an object is:
A. The more molecules it has
B. The faster its molecules vibrate
C. The smaller it becomes
D. None of the above

4. When next to colder air, hot air:
A. Rises
B. Takes up less space
C. Is a form of Conduction
D. All of the above

5. Heat always flows from:
A. Top to bottom
B. Warmer areas to cooler areas
C. South to north

6. Which of the following is NOT a form of heat transfer:
A. Radiation
B. Conduction
C. Convention

7. The Sun produces different kinds of light, including: _____,
_____, and _____.

8. Infrared light is also called _____.

9. Dark colors absorb more:
A. Light
B. Heat
C. Energy
D. All of the above

10. White surfaces _____ light; black surfaces _____ light.

11. The greatest amount of energy is absorbed when light strikes an object:
A. From the north
B. At a 90 degree angle
C. In the summer

12. After it is absorbed into an object, light turns into _____.

13. Conduction is the movement of heat through_____.

14. Convection currents transfer heat in:
A. Fluids
B. Water
C. Air
D. All of the above

15. A spotlight is shining onto black paper. Energy is being transferred by

_____.

16. If air is standing still, it transfers heat:
A. Slowly
B. Quickly
C. Not at all

17. Materials that trap air and and keep convection currents from forming are good:
A. Conductors
B. Radiators
C. Insulators
D. None of the above.

3 Solar Ovens

How to Cook Food With The Sun

Have you ever been inside a greenhouse? Greenhouses are made of see-through materials like glass or plastic. They're used to grow heat-loving plants during the winter. They do this by trapping both the heat energy and the visible light energy from the sun.

Much of the Sun's heat is absorbed by the Earth's atmosphere, and doesn't make it to the Earth's surface. Visible light passes through the atmosphere more easily than heat does.

Visible light also passes easily through the glass of the greenhouse. It's absorbed by the plants and structures inside, and changes into heat. Heat (infrared radiation) doesn't pass out through the glass as easily as visible light passes in.

Greenhouses trap the sun's heat.

The heat stays trapped inside the greenhouse. The glass walls also slow the movement of air between the inside and the outside, and decrease the loss of heat by convection.

This is called the **greenhouse effect**, and we can use it to cook food with sunlight. To do this we need to remember all the things we've learned so far:

1. Sunlight is absorbed by dark-colored surfaces, and turns into heat.

2. Sunlight is reflected by white and mirror-like surfaces.

3. Glass lets sunlight in more easily than it lets heat out.

4. Facing the sun directly gives more solar energy.

5. Insulation slows heat flow.

A Solar Box Cooker

Solar Box Coookers can reach 400 degrees

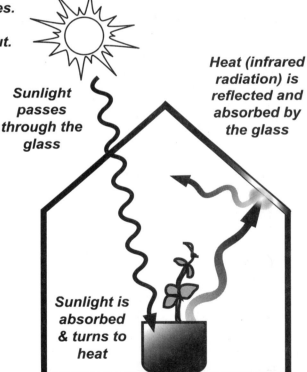

Sunlight passes through the glass

Heat (infrared radiation) is reflected and absorbed by the glass

Sunlight is absorbed & turns to heat

The Greenhouse Effect in buildings

A box can make a great solar oven. A transparent top lets sunlight in, and black surfaces inside absorb the light and turn it into heat. We can also use reflectors to focus more sunlight inside, and insulation can keep the box from losing too much heat.

Principles of Solar Cooking

Remember: **NEVER LOOK DIRECTLY AT THE SUN!**

The basic ideas of solar cooking can be remembered with the word **"BAKE"**

B stands for: "Bring in" *as much sunlight as possible.*

To bring as much sunlight as possible into a solar cooker, keep the top facing toward the sun. You might need to turn the box during cooking to follow the sun.

Reflectors also bring more light in. Mirrors, aluminum foil and certain types of metallic paint can be used to make reflectors.

A stands for: "Absorb" *energy from sunlight.*

Remember: Much of the Sun's heat is absorbed by the Earth's atmosphere. Visible light reaches the Earth's surface more easily.

We need to absorb heat from the Sun. We also need to absorb visible light, and change it into heat inside the cooker. To do this, make sure the bottom of the box is black to absorb both visible and infrared light.

Using a black pot to hold the food also helps absorb more energy from the sun.

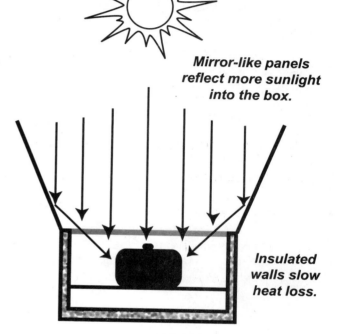

Mirror-like panels reflect more sunlight into the box.

Insulated walls slow heat loss.

Black cookware and bottom tray inside the box absorb heat.

K stands for: "Keep" *the heat inside the cooker.*

The glass (or clear plastic) top lets sunlight in better than it lets heat out.

If the box is sealed tightly, it will also be hard for air currents to carry away heat by convection or infiltration..

If the walls are insulated, heat loss by conduction will be slowed down too. Different materials like crumpled paper, cardboard and fiberglass are used for insulation in solar cookers. These methods help the oven get hotter and cook more quickly. The food will also keep cooking if clouds block the sun for a little while.

Got Sunglasses?

E stands for: "Eat & Enjoy" *the food cooked by the sun!*

Solar History

In ancient China, the son in charge of lighting the stove carried a curved mirror in his belt. He used this to start a fire by focusing sunlight onto kindling. Europeans in the time of Leonardo da Vinci lit the family stove in the same way.

The first meal in history cooked only with sunlight was made by Horace de Saussure in 1767. He heated soup in an insulated box topped with several layers of glass.

In the 1830's, Sir John Herschel used a similar solar oven to cook a "very respectable stew of meat". This meal was eaten "with no small relish by the entertained bystanders" at the Cape of Good Hope in South Africa.

French Foreign Legionnaires in North Africa in the 1870's had no fuel to cook with except sunlight. They used a different kind of solar oven designed by Augustin Mouchot. This cooker used a cylindrical pot inside a reflector shaped like a lampshade.

Mouchot's sun oven could be adjusted throughout the day to keep it facing the sun. It was also collapsible, so the soldiers could easily take it with them on their famously long marches.

Using his portable solar oven, Mouchot baked a pound of bread in 45 minutes, and boiled over two pounds of potatoes in one hour. He also cooked a roast "whose juices sizzled to the bottom" in less than half an hour.

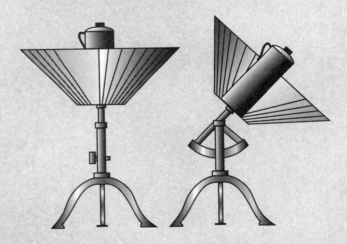

Mouchot's concentrator solar cooker

This type of oven is called a **concentrator solar cooker**. Concentrator cookers can reach much higher temperatures than solar box cookers. Mouchot made one model that could melt tin, lead, and zinc in a matter of minutes.

Projects #5   Pizza Box Solar Oven

Try out these ideas by making your own solar oven using a pizza box, tin foil and a plastic oven bag. This oven can bake brownies with sunlight.

Pizza Box Solar Oven

Review Questions

1. Glass rooms let sunlight in more easily than than they let _____ out.

2. The greenhouse effect:
A. Doesn't work in solar ovens
B. Uses conduction
C. Traps infrared radiation (heat)
D. All of the above.

3. The inside of a solar oven uses _____ surfaces to absorb heat.

4. To bring more sunlight into a solar cooker:
A. Use reflectors
B. Face north
C. Use insulation

5. To keep heat from escaping through the bottom and sides, a solar oven uses:
A. Reflectors
B. Insulation
C. A transparent top
D. All of the above

6. When using a solar oven it's important to:
A. Not look directly at the Sun.
B. Keep the oven pointed directly at the Sun.
C. Use potholders
D. All of the above

7. To reduce heat loss by convection, be sure to:
A. Seal the oven tightly
B. Point the oven toward the south
C. Bake in the middle of the day
D. None of the above.

8. _____ passes more easily through glass than infrared light does.

9. _____ solar cookers can reach much higher temperatures than solar box cookers.

10. In the 1800s, Augutin Mouchot made a solar cooker that could melt
A. Tin
B. Lead
C. Zinc
D. All of the above

4 Solar Hot Water

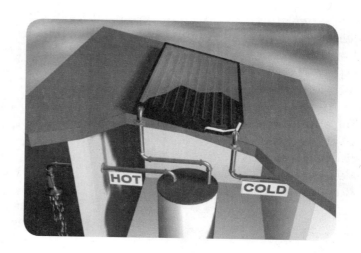

Heating Water With Sunlight

We use hot water for many different things, like bathing, cleaning our clothes and washing the dishes. Heating this water with fossil fuels is not only harmful to the environment, it's expensive.

About 14% of the energy used by the average american household goes to heating water, according to the U.S. Department of Energy.

Fortunately, the same principles we used to heat food in solar ovens can be used to heat water in our houses. To see how, let's start by looking at the way we usually heat water.

water heater

Standard Water Heaters

The hot water we use in our homes comes from a big tank called a **water heater**.

The water heater uses a gas burner (or an electric element) to heat water. As the water warms up, it rises to the top of the tank.

When a hot water faucet is opened, cold water flows into the bottom of the tank and pushes hot water out the top.

Inside view of standard gas water heater

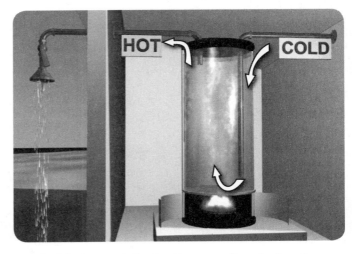

HOT   COLD

Cold water at the bottom pushes hot water out the top.

Solar Batch Water Heaters

HOT   COLD

Breadbox water heater

One of the easiest ways to heat water with sunlight is to paint a water heater tank black, and put it outside in an insulated box. This is one kind of solar batch heater, called a **breadbox heater**.

The front and top of the "breadbox" are made of glass. Hinged reflectors are attached, and can be closed at night to keep the tank warm.

The cold water flows through the breadbox heater first, and then into the standard water heater. This way the Sun preheats the water, and the standard water heater adds heat if the water from the breadbox isn't hot enough.

Solar Collectors

Unfortunately, heating a whole tank of water in the sun takes a long time, often all day.

One way to heat water more quickly is to use a *solar collector*.

Solar collectors run liquid through several thin tubes instead of one big tank. This provides more surface area to absorb sunlight.

Have you noticed how hot the water can get in a garden hose left in the Sun? This is the same principle used in solar collectors.

Project #7   Soda Can Breadbox Heater

Make your own solar water heater using a soda can.

Solar for Swimming Pools

Swimming pools use a lot of energy. According to the U.S. Department of Energy, hundreds of billions of cubic feet of natural gas are consumed each year to heat the nation's pools.

There are several ways to heat pools with solar energy. One of the simplest is to pump pool water through a black plastic pipe with several bends in it.

This pipe heats water quickly, but it's not surrounded by glass, so the water doesn't get as hot as it could (which is fine for heating pool water).

Plastic pipe solar collector for swimming pool

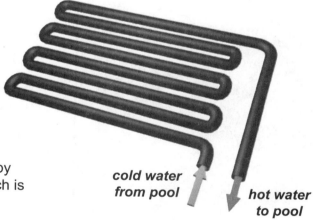

cold water from pool

hot water to pool

Flat Plate Collectors

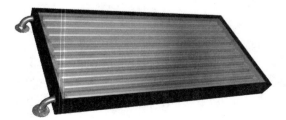

flat plate solar collector

A *flat plate solar collector* is more efficient. It uses thin metal tubes attached to a black-colored metal sheet. The whole system is put in an insulated glass covered box.

The black metal sheet (or *flat plate*) absorbs heat too, and conducts it to the pipes.

There are several types of flat plate collectors, and many ways to connect them to household water systems.

Using Solar Collectors in Warm Climates

In places where winters are mild, and freezing is not a problem, a solar collector can be attached directly to the water heater.

The cold water enters the solar collector at the bottom, is warmed by the Sun, and rises to the top.

Now when hot water is drawn out of the standard water heater, it's replaced by preheated water from the solar collector.

The problem with this system is that the hot water stays in the collector until a faucet opens. The water in the collector gets very hot, but the heat is not transferred to the water heater tank. To make the system more effective, it is necessary to circulate the solar heat to the water tank.

Cutaway view of flat plate collector

The solar collector preheats the water.

Thermosiphon Systems

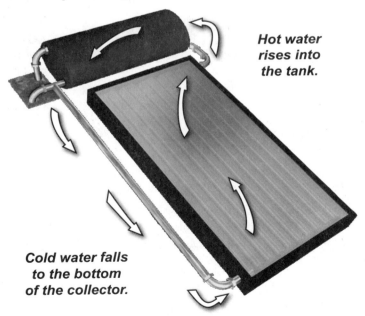

Hot water rises into the tank.

Cold water falls to the bottom of the collector.

Thermosiphon systems place the tank above the collector.

The simplest way to keep water flowing between the collector and the tank is to use a **thermosiphon system**.

In this system a water tank is attached **above** the solar collector.

Now as the sun heats the water, it rises out of the top of the collector into the tank. Cold water falls from the tank to the bottom of the collector, and a convection loop forms.

A thermosiphon system circulates the water without using a pump.

Remember that all of these systems only work in places where the weather is warm. If the temperature outside is below freezing, the water in the pipes can freeze too.

Solar Collectors in Cold Climates

Drainback system

On winter nights, and cold, cloudy winter days, the water in the solar collector can freeze. This will stop the water from moving, and can also damage the pipes.

This is because water does an unusual thing when it freezes: it actually expands a little. One way to make sure this doesn't happen is to drain the water from the collector when the weather is cold.

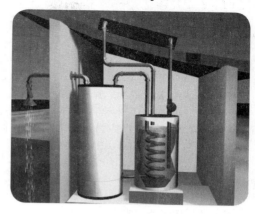

Cutaway view showing heat exchanger

Drainback Systems

A **drainback system** uses two separate tanks. One tank is connected to the solar collector. An electric pump pushes the water from this tank through the collector. When the water reaches the top of the collector it falls (or **drains back**) to the tank. This is the drainback tank.

The second tank is a standard water heater. The water in this heater doesn't mix with the water in the drainback tank. Instead, it passes through a metal coil inside the drainback tank. The coil acts as a heat exchanger, and transfers heat from the drainback tank to the water heater.

When the weather is too cold, the collector pump shuts off. Gravity causes the water to drain back from the collector to the tank. Now there's no water left in the collector to freeze.

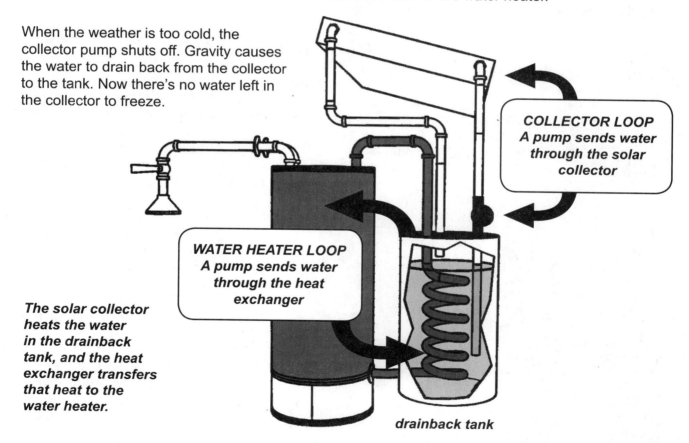

COLLECTOR LOOP
A pump sends water through the solar collector

WATER HEATER LOOP
A pump sends water through the heat exchanger

The solar collector heats the water in the drainback tank, and the heat exchanger transfers that heat to the water heater.

drainback tank

A drainback system drains the water from the collecter when the weather freezes.

Tankless Water Heaters

Whether or not they're connected to solar collectors, standard water heaters still waste energy. This is because water is kept hot all the time, even when it's not being used. This is like keeping a car running all the time, even when no one is driving it.

Remember: heat is always moving from hotter areas to cooler areas. Although a water heater may be insulated, it's still losing heat to the outside air.

A more efficient way to heat water is by using a demand or **tankless water heater**.

Tankless water heater

Heat Exchangers

Instead of a big tank of water, gas-fired tankless water heaters use a metal coil called a **heat exchanger**.

When a hot water faucet opens, a gas burner lights, and rapidly heats the water as it flows through the coil.

The coil is made of an excellent conductor, such as copper. The moving water rapidly absorbs the heat from the pipe.

Inside view of tankless water heater

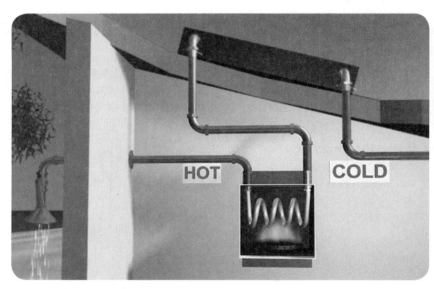

The burner heats water as it flows through the heat exchanger.

Cutaway solar collector attached to tankless heater

Solar Preheat

Some types of tankless water heaters can even be attached to solar collectors.

This way the sun can preheat the water before it goes through the heat exchanger.

Solar History

It may surprise you that the first commercial solar water heater went on the market in 1891. Clarence Kemp invented and sold it through his Baltimore appliance factory outlet.

Kemp had seen earlier solar water heaters put together by farmers—metal water tanks painted black and placed directly in the sun out in the fields during the summer. By late afternoon, when farm work had everyone's skin full of grit, grime, and sweat, and their bodies exhausted, farmhands opened up the spigot on the tank, and filled buckets with water hot enough to soothe their aching muscles and refresh their overheated bodies.

The problem with these simple solar heaters, Kemp observed, was not whether they could produce hot water, but when and for how long. Even on clear, hot days, it usually took from morning to early afternoon for the water to get hot. And as soon as the sun set, the tanks rapidly lost heat because they were uninsulated and unprotected from the cool night air.

Kemp had also read in popular journals how the American astrophysicist Samuel Pierpoint Langley had taken an insulated, glass-covered box and exposed it to the sun on the snow-covered slopes of Mount Whitney. Though outside temperatures had dropped below freezing, the inside of the box heated up above the boiling point of water. Kemp realized that if he placed several tanks painted black inside a glass-covered box, he would have a superior method of heating water with the sun. In 1891, he won a patent for the new heater, and called it the Climax, the world's first commercial solar water heater.

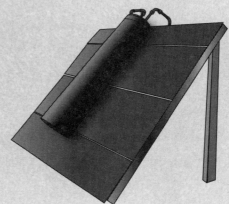

The first solar water heaters were bare metal tanks painted black.

He advertised his heater as "the acme of simplicity" compared with conventional water heaters. Just turn on the faucet and "instantly out comes the hot water," the sales literature boasted. Thanks to the Climax, according to company brochures, housewives no longer had to fire up the stove in summer, and wealthy gentlemen, who had to stay behind to work while their families and servants left sultry Baltimore to summer in more pleasant climes, could return home at night and instantly draw hot water with no fuss or bother.

Sales of the Climax really took off in California. By 1897, one-third of households in Pasadena relied on the Climax for heating water. More than 1,600 were sold in southern California by 1900. Economics was the prime lure of the Climax. For an investment of $25, the owner saved about $9 a year on coal. As one journalist pointed out, exorbitant fuel prices forced Californians "to take the asset of sunshine into full partnership. In this section of the country where soft coal sells for $13 a ton (and the huge peaches bring only $2 a ton), a builder cannot afford to waste his sun-rays. California is in particular need of its solar heaters."

Climax Solar-Water Heater
UTILIZING ONE OF NATURE'S GENEROUS FORCES
THE SUN'S HEAT { Stored up in Hot Water for Baths, Domestic and other Purposes.
GIVES HOT WATER at all HOURS OF THE DAY AND NIGHT.
NO DELAY.
FLOWS INSTANTLY.
NO CARE. —— NO WORRY.
ALWAYS CHARGED. ALWAYS READY.
THE WATER AT TIMES ALMOST BOILS.
Price, No. 1, $25.00
This Size will Supply sufficient for 3 to 5 Baths.
CLARENCE M. KEMP, BALTIMORE, MD.

Price Of No 1 Heater for 1892 Required to $1?????

Daily Gifts

Others, though, saw a more important reason for going solar. Charles Pope, writing in 1903, urged consumers to "consider that wood and oil and coal and gas are steadily consumed by use. Not only will the coming generations be less comfortably supplied—a thing most of us care very little about—but the drain today may produce distress in our own homes and lay an embargo on our own business tomorrow. Contrast this with the freedom of the people who receive daily gifts of fuel from the Creator, taking all they wish, all they can use, freely."

Clarence M. Kemp Inventor of the Climax solar collector

Between 1898 and 1909, more than a dozen inventors filed patents for new solar water heaters, but everyone merely refined the Climax design. In 1909, William J. Bailey saw the shortcomings of the glass-covered tank solar water heaters—collecting and storing solar heated water in the same unit allowed the water to cool down after dark or when the weather got bad.

Bailey revolutionized the solar water heater industry by separating the solar collector from the storage unit. He attached narrow water pipes to a black metal plate and put them into a shallow, glass-covered, insulated box. Then he connected the collector to an elevated, autonomous, insulated storage unit. As the sun heated the water, it became lighter than the colder water below, naturally rising into the storage tank. His solar water heater worked better than Kemp's because the sun heated a smaller volume of water at a time, and the heated water immediately went to a storage tank protected from the elements.

Bailey called his company the Day and Night Solar Heater Company, because unlike the Climax, it supplied solar heated water during the day and at night. The added benefits of the Day and Night soon put those manufacturing the Climax out of business. By the end of World War I, more than 4,000 households in southern California heated their water with Day and Night solar water heaters.

Cheap Gas & Electricity

The discovery of cheap local supplies of natural gas concurrent with the development of the thermostatically controlled gas water heater in the early 1920s killed the solar water heater industry in southern California. The solar water heater business then migrated to southern Florida, where a booming housing market and high energy costs created much demand for Bailey's invention. By 1941, more than half the households in Miami heated their water with the sun. But war came, the government froze the use of copper, and the solar water heater industry came to an

William J. Bailey, founder of the Day & Night Solar Heater Company

abrupt halt. Solar water heating took off again after the war, but cheap electric rates, combined with aggressive sales of electric water heaters by the utilities, stymied new growth. The once thriving Floridian solar water heater industry was reduced to a small service business by 1955. The two oil embargoes of the 1970s encouraged new interest in solar water heating. Subsequent sharp drops in fossil fuel prices, combined with the end of tax credits for purchasing solar water heaters, once again put a damper on the American solar water heater industry.

Ahead of Us

Other parts of the world have enthusiastically embraced Bailey's invention. Millions of Japanese have purchased solar water heaters. More than ninety percent of Israelis heat their water with the sun. In Europe, so many people use solar water heaters like the Day and Night design that they save the equivalent of the energy produced by five large nuclear power plants. Most never imagined that the technology they use dates back so far and comes from California!

John Perlin

Review Questions

1. A black water tank inside a glass-covered box is called a

_____ heater.

2. Flat plate solar collectors heat water with:
A. Solar electricity
B. Several tubes
C. Condensation

3. Water flows between a solar collector and a storage tank without a pump in a

_____ system.

4. Where must the storage tank be in the system in Question #3?
A. In the attic
B. On the roof
C. Above the solar collector

4. Systems where the solar collector is attached directly to a water heater are NOT recommended:
A. For swimming pools
B. In freezing climates
C. For flat plate collectors
D. None of the above

5. A _____ system uses two separate tanks.

6. What moves liquid between the tank and the solar collector in the system in Question #5?
A. Gravity
B. A pump
C. A & B
D. None of the above

7. Water does an unusual thing when it freezes. It _____.

8. A water heater that heats water only when a faucet is on is called a:
A. Breadbox heater
B. Flatplate collector
C. Tankless heater

9. A _____ is a device (often a metal coil) that transfers heat between fluids that aren't in direct contact.

10. The first solar water heaters in the U.S. were just black painted_____ .

11. The first commercial solar water heater, the Climax, was patented in:
A. 1891
B. 1924
C. 1972

12. The first commercial solar water heaters were better than many home-built solar water heaters because they were:
A. Covered with glass
B. Facing south
C. On metal sheets
D. All of the above

13. The Day and Night solar heater had:
A. Narrow pipes on a metal plate
B. An insulated glass-covered box
C. A separate storage tank
D. All of the above

5 Passive Solar Design

How to Stay Comfortable All Year Long

Most homes burn fossil fuels to stay warm in the winter and use air conditioners in the summer. *Passive solar home design* uses knowledge of the sun to heat buildings in the winter and keep them cool in the summer.

Passive solar home designers do this by using the ideas we've already explored in earlier chapters.

1. Position the house to use the Sun's Energy

In the northern hemisphere the sun is in the southern sky.

The single most important method for using solar energy is to orient the building to capture sunlight.

For home heating, this means aiming windows toward the south. It's usually better to have the longer side of the building facing south.

The landscape around a building can also be used to help heat and cool the building. Trees and hills can give protection from the sun and weather.

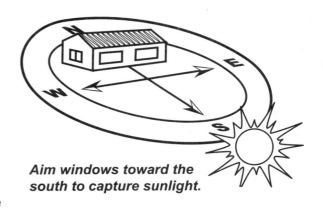

Aim windows toward the south to capture sunlight.

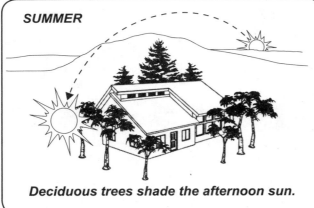

Deciduous trees shade the afternoon sun.

Some trees (called *deciduous* trees) drop their leaves in the winter. They can shade the house in summer, and let sunlight in during winter. On the west side, deciduous trees can block heat from the low afternoon summer sun.

Trees and bushes which keep their leaves all year are called *evergreens*.

On the north side, evergreens can protect the house from harsh weather, and winter winds.

Hills on the north side of the house can also give protection from winter weather.

Before building, passive solar designers often spend time at the building site, paying attention to the Sun, wind and weather.

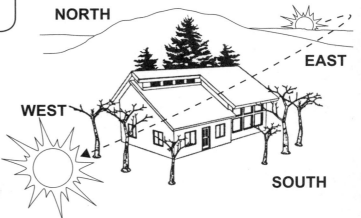

IN WINTER, bare deciduous trees let sunlight in.

2. Use South Facing Windows to Bring in Sunlight

The simplest passive solar design is called **suntempering**. Suntempering just adds windows to the south side of a house.

Designing a house with south-facing glass is an easy and effective way to heat with sunlight, and often adds very little to the cost of the home.

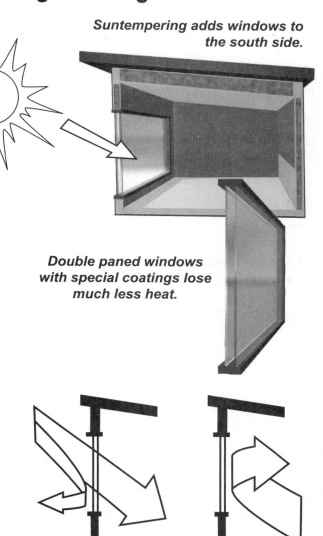

Suntempering adds windows to the south side.

Windows do lose heat

Even though infrared radiation doesn't pass easily through them, windows do lose heat.

In fact, an average window can lose several times as much heat as the same area of wall. That's why you often feel colder when you stand near a window.

Remember the greenhouse effect: sunlight passes in through the window glass, is absorbed inside the house, and turns to heat.

Much of this heat doesn't pass out through the window, but is absorbed by the glass. The glass itself heats up, and then it transfers heat to the outside.

Many newer windows are designed to transfer heat more slowly. They often use two panes of glass with a space in between. The space acts as an insulator.

Double paned windows with special coatings lose much less heat.

Low-e glass lets most of the Sun's heat in, and keeps more heat from escaping.

Some windows use a special kind of glass, called **low-e glass**. Low-e glass has an invisible, thin metal coating that reflects heat.

Low-e glass used for passive solar design lets most of the Sun's heat enter the house. Once inside, this heat is reflected from the glass. The glass stays cooler, and transfers less heat to the outside.

Put fewer windows on the north side

Windows on the north side of a house can lose a lot of heat, and get very little useful sunlight in the winter. Passive solar designs usually have few north facing windows.

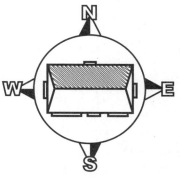

Use as few windows on the north as possible.

3. Keep Heat Inside with Insulation

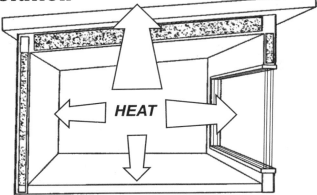

Houses lose heat through the roof, walls, and floor too.

Insulation slows down these heat losses.

Heat rises: use more insulation under the roof.

Insulation

Adding insulation to the walls, ceiling and floors makes it harder for heat to escape from a house. Because heat rises, it's very important to insulate the roof and ceiling. The thicker the insulation is, the more time it takes for the building to cool down.

Insulation is made from many different things, like fiberglass, paper fiber, and special plastics like Styrofoam.

These things work like the down stuffing in sleeping bags. They have thousands of tiny spaces that trap air. The trapped air keeps convection currents from forming, and slows down conduction. Reflective coverings like aluminum foil can stop heat loss by radiation too.

It's important to seal cracks by windows and doors to stop drafts. A lot of heat can be lost by air flowing quickly through small holes. This is called *infiltration*, and it can be a major source of heat loss. New houses often put a thin layer of plastic between the walls to stop air and moisture.

Even with the best insulation, a house will cool down. The colder it is outside, the faster a house will cool down.

4. Store Heat with Thermal Mass

Have you noticed after a hot day that the sidewalk stays warm at night? That's because the sidewalk has a large amount of *thermal mass*.

Thermal mass is the ability of an object to absorb and store heat. Dense materials like stone and water have high thermal mass.

They can absorb large amounts of sunlight in the day, and turn it into heat. At night, the stored heat is released.

Thermal mass is just the opposite of insulation. Insulation has many tiny air spaces, thermal mass has hardly any. This means heat can be conducted into the mass and stored.

A boulder heats up during the day and releases heat at night.

Direct Gain Systems

Another common passive solar design is a **direct gain** system. It uses south facing windows like the suntempered house, and adds thermal mass inside to store heat.

The mass heats up during the day, and releases that heat into the room at night.

Walls and floors of concrete or stone are often used for thermal mass, but many other materials store heat well too.

Bricks, tile, adobe and even water can be used as thermal mass. Water must be put in sturdy containers, but it can absorb about twice as much heat as stone.

Direct gain systems are simple and low cost, and can take advantage of materials used in many standard homes: windows and concrete.

A thermal mass wall absorbs the sun's heat during the day...

...and releases that heat into the room at night.

Sunspaces

Some passive solar designs separate the windowed area from the rest of the house. This glassed in room is called a **sunspace,** or **solar greenhouse**.

Sunspaces are **isolated gain systems** because sunlight is collected in an area which can be closed off from the rest of the house.

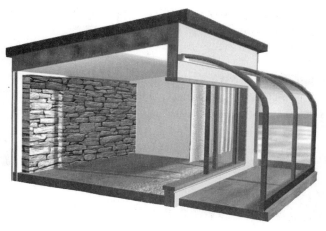

Sunspaces can supply a lot of heat to a house, but are often too hot to be in.

Thermal mass is used to store solar energy in the sunspace. Doors or windows next to the sunspace can be opened during the day to let heat move into the house by convection.

Because of the large amount of glass, sunspaces heat up very quickly during the day, and lose heat quickly after sunset. They may get too hot during the day, and are often closed off from the rest of the house at night.

It's usually better to have a solid and well insulated roof over the sunspace. Although glass roofs collect more sunlight, they also lose more heat during the night. And they can cause overheating in warm weather. Thick curtains, or movable window insulation will also slow heat loss at night.

Trombe Walls

Trombe walls were developed by a frenchman named Felix Trombe (Trombe rhymes with Tom).

A Trombe wall is just a thermal mass wall placed directly behind a south facing window.

The wall is usually painted black, and has vents or windows at the top and bottom.

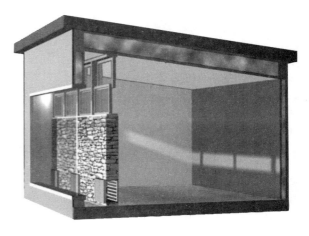

A trombe wall is a mass wall behind a window.

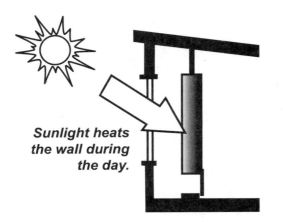

Sunlight heats the wall during the day.

During the day, the house acts like a solar collector, and the Trombe wall captures the sun's energy.

It takes several hours for the sun to heat the wall, and the room behind it stays cool.

If the room needs to be heated during the day, the vents in the wall can be opened.

Daytime heating

With the wall vents open, convection currents carry heat into the room.

As air between the window and the wall heats up it rises, and passes into the room.

Cooler air near the floor moves into the space left by the rising hot air.

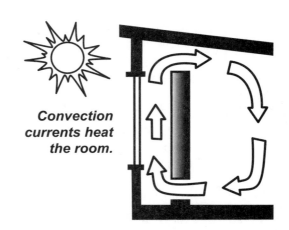

Convection currents heat the room.

Nighttime heating

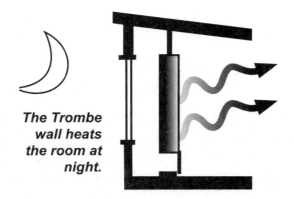

The Trombe wall heats the room at night.

The heat of the sun works its way slowly through the wall by conduction.

During the evening, the inside of the wall is warm, and begins to radiate heat into the room.

The vents in the wall are closed to keep heat from escaping through the window.

5. Keep Cool with Convection Currents

Nighttime cooling

The simplest way to cool a passive solar home is to open windows and vents at night.

Thermal mass can then radiate heat to the outside. Hot air rising through ceiling vents will draw cooler air into the house. This air will absorb heat from a mass floor or wall.

The next day the mass will be a source of "coolth", and absorb heat from the inside of the house. If the south facing windows are covered and shaded, the house often stays cool through the heat of the day.

Open windows and vents let heat escape at night.

Daytime cooling

Escaping hot air draws cooler air into the house.

Mass walls are also used to bring cooler air into the house during the day.

To do this, outside vents are placed above the mass wall. Low vents are placed on the cooler north side of the house.

Hot air rising past the mass wall is then vented to the outside. This draws cooler air into the building through the north side vents.

Earth cooling

Another way to cool with convection is by drawing outside air through tubes buried in the ground.

Tubes made of good conductors are buried several feet underground to avoid the warm daytime surface temperature.

As rising hot air leaves the building, it draws outside air in. The outside air transfers heat to the cool earth as it moves through the tubes, and cools the house as it enters.

The earth cools incoming air.

6. Enjoy Natural Light with Daylighting

Sunlight in your home does much more than provide heat. Natural light can make a house more comfortable, brighten your mood and, according to the U.S. Department of Energy, may even inprove your health and productivity. Using sunlight to light our buildings also reduces the energy needed for electric lights.

But the glare of too much direct sunlight is uncomfortable, and can overheat a house, especially in the summer. Good daylighting balances natural lighting with solar heating.

Daylighting is not the same as sunlighting. **Daylighting** is the practice of bringing soft, indirect sunlight into buildings, and reducing the direct sun's heat and glare.

Indirect sunlight is sunlight that's reflected into a room, or filtered through a white translucent skylight or window. Sunlight is often reflected off the ceiling to imitate the soft light of the sky.

Indirect sunlight also comes through windows on the north (or shady) side of the house, and through windows protected by overhangs.

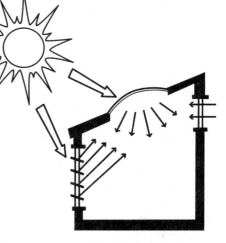

Daylighting uses indirect sunlight.

Overhangs

With overhangs, a window can get soft, indirect light in the summer, and also receive direct sunlight in the winter for solar heating. Overhangs can also be used as light shelves to reflect light deeper into a room. (See next page.)

Overhangs are sections of the roof that "hang over" windows, and shade them from the hot summer sun. They are also called eaves. Cloth awnings can be used for this purpose too.

Overhangs block the direct light from the high summer sun, but still let indirect sunlight into the house.

Because of the Earth's tilt, the sun doesn't rise as high in the sky during the winter. This means that properly sized overhangs will let the sunlight in when it's needed most: in the winter.

A simple overhang can shade noon-time sunlight in the summer, but it might not let light deep into the room. One way to do both is to use light shelves.

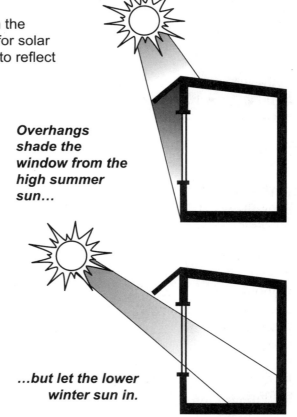

Overhangs shade the window from the high summer sun...

...but let the lower winter sun in.

Light Shelves

One of the best ways to use daylighting is to bounce sunlight off the ceiling. This brings a soft, even light deep into the room. Light shelves can do this well.

A *light shelf* is a flat overhang put above eye-level over a south-facing window. Above this overhang is a small window. The light shelf protects the lower window from the summer sun, and also reflects light through the small window onto the ceiling.

Light shelves reflect light onto the ceiling.

Curtains & Blinds

Curtains and blinds can soften natural sunlight, and be adjusted to provide different amounts of light. They also slow heat transfer by radiation, and can keep the house cooler in the summer.

Thin curtains will let some indirect sunlight into the room, yet still reduce heat gain. A *valance* or box along the top also helps slow convection currents behind the curtain.

Wide slat blinds reflect direct sunlight up to the ceiling and walls, providing soft natural light and stopping bright glare.

Adjustable blinds also let direct sunlight in when and where you want it, perhaps in a kitchen breakfast nook.

In the winter curtains and blinds can slow heat *lost* through the windows, and keep the house warmer.

Curtains soften direct sunlight.

Blinds reflect sunlight up into the room.

Skylights

Skylights are windows in the roof. White translucent skylights are not see-through, but they do let light in. They also block heat.

If you use a clear skylight, make sure it has a special low-e coating that blocks most of the heat from the sun. Without this coating, clear skylights would be a poor choice, because they let in a large amount of heat in the summer, when the sun is high in the sky. They also lose heat in the winter.

Skylights that open and close can be used to vent summer heat as it rises to the ceiling.

White translucent skylights let in light and block heat.

Tubular Skylights

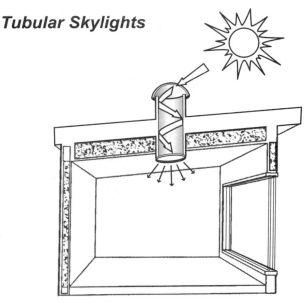

Tubular skylights reflect sunlight from the roof to the inside of the house through a long shiny tube.

At the end of the tube is a white or prismatic diffuser.

The diffuser blocks heat and spreads the light out evenly.

Tubular skylights are an inexpensive way to bring natural sunlight into rooms with few or no windows, through an attic.

Tubular skylights reflect sunlight into the house.

Clerestory Windows

Clerestory windows are used to bring light deep into a building. They're placed high on the wall, and let sunlight shine on the ceiling. This gives a pleasant light, similar to the light of the sky.

Sometimes daylighting seems to work against passive solar heating. For example, a north-facing clerestory might be used for non-glare indirect light, but for solar heating you'd face the clerestory south.

The art in passive solar design balances good daylighting with passive solar heating.

South-facing clerestory provides direct sunlight for solar heat.

North-facing clerestory gives indirect light without heat.

Solar History

The 5th Century

During the fifth century BC., the Greeks faced severe fuel shortages. Fortunately, an alternative source of energy was available - the sun. Archaeological evidence shows that a standard house plan evolved during the fifth century so that every house, whether rural or urban, could make maximum use of the sun's warm rays during winter.

Those living in ancient Greece confirm what archaeologists have found. Aristotle noted, builders made sure to shelter the north side of the house to keep out the cold winter winds. And Socrates, who lived in a solar-heated house, observed, "In houses that look toward the south, the sun penetrates the portico in winter" which keeps the house heated in winter.

The great playwright Aeschylus went so far as to assert that only primitives and barbarians "lacked knowledge of houses turned to face the winter sun, dwelling beneath the ground like swarming ants in sunless caves."

The ancient Greeks planned whole cities in Greece and Asia Minor such as Priene, shown in the illustration, to allow every homeowner access to sunlight during winter to warm their homes.

By running the streets in a checkerboard pattern running east-west and north-south every home could face south, permitting the winter sun to flow into the house throughout the day.

Ancient Rome

Fuel consumption in ancient Rome was even more profligate than in Classical Greece. In architecture, the Romans remedied the problem in the same fashion as did the Greeks.

Vitruvius, the preeminent Roman architectural writer of the 1st century BC., advised builders in the Italian peninsula, "Buildings should be thoroughly shut in rather than exposed toward the north, and the main portion should face the warmer south side." Varro, a contemporary of Vitruvius, verified that most houses of at least the Roman upper class followed Vitruvius' advice, stating, "What men of our day aim at is to have their winter rooms face the falling sun [southwest]."

The Romans improved on Greek solar architecture by covering south-facing windows with clear materials such as mica or glass. They also passed sun-right laws that forbade other builders from blocking a solar-designed structure's access to the winter sun.

Cross section of a Roman heliocaminus. The term means "sun furnace." The Romans used the term to describe their south-facing rooms.

They became much hotter in winter than similarly oriented Greek homes because the Romans covered their window spaces with mica or glass while the Greeks did not.

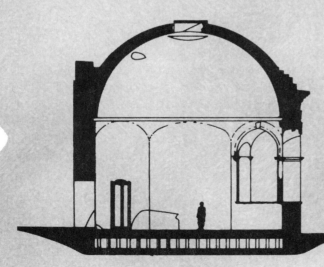

Clear materials like mica or glass act as solar heat traps: they readily admit sunlight into a room but hold in the heat that accumulates inside.

So the temperature inside a glazed window would rise well above what was possible in a Greek solar oriented home, making the heliocaminus truly a "sun furnace" when compared to its Greek counterpart.

Solar Greenhouses

Like the ancient Romans, the 18th century Dutch and others in Europe at the time, used glass-covered south-facing greenhouses to capture solar heat in wintertime to keep their exotic plants warm.

To prevent the solar heat captured during the day from escaping, the Dutch covered the glass at night with canvas coverings.

The ancient Romans not only used window coverings to hold in solar heat for their homes but also relied on such solar heat traps for horticulture so that plants would mature quicker, produce fruits and vegetables out of season, and allow for the cultivation at home of exotic plants from hotter climates.

With the fall of the Roman Empire, so too came the collapse of glass for either buildings or greenhouses. Only with the revival of trade during the 16th century came renewed interest in growing in solar-heated greenhouses exotics brought back from the newly-discovered lands of the East Indies and the Americas. Trade also created expendable incomes that allowed the freedom to take up such genteel pursuits as horticulture once more.

John Perlin

Review Questions

1. _____trees may block the summer Sun, but not the winter Sun.

2. Trees and bushes that protect against winter winds are called _____.

3. Adding windows to the south side of a house is the simplest type of passive solar design, and is called:
A. Suntempering
B. South-facing
C. Orientation

4. Glass with a special coating to slow heat loss is called:
A. Double pane glass
B. Low-e glass
C. Passive solar glass
D. All of the above

5. To slow heat transfer, it's important to insulate:
A. Walls
B. Floors
C. Ceiling
D. All of the above

6. Air leaking through cracks and spaces by doors and windows, is called _____.

7. Thermal mass is the ability of an object to _____ and _____ heat.

8. Which has greater thermal mass?
A. Stone
B. Styrofoam
C. Water

9. A solar design using south facing glass and thermal mass floors is called a

_____system.

10. An isolated gain system uses:
A. A sunspace (or solar greenhouse)
B. Summer winds
C. Drainback systems
D. All of the above

11. A thermal mass wall placed directly behind south facing glass is called a

_____.

12. The heat of the Sun works its way slowly through thermal mass by:

_____.

13. Convection cooling with a Trombe wall uses:
A. High outside vents near the top of the Trombe wall
B. Low vents on the cooler side of the house
C. Low vents in the Trombe wall
D. All of the above

14. The part of the roof that shades windows is called an

_____.

15. Ancient Greeks took advantage of solar energy by:
A. Using glass
B. Suntempering
C. Facing buildings south
D. All of the above

16. Houses that use daylighting can include:
A. Tubular skylights
B. Wide slat blinds
C. Clerestory windows
D. All of the above

6 Solar Electricity

Making Electricity with Photovoltaics

Light energy can be turned directly into electricity. The device that does this is called a ***photovoltaic cell***. It's also called a solar cell, or a PV cell. The term photovolatic combines ***photo***, from the Greek word for light, with ***voltaic,*** named after Alessandro Volta, a pioneer in the science of electricity.

Photovoltaic Cell

Photovoltaic cells have no moving parts, and run silently, without polluting the environment. They are made of semiconductor materials like silicon, the most common element in the Earth's crust.

The silicon in PV cells is chemically treated to make a postive and a negative layer. Between these two layers an electrical field is created, similar to a battery.

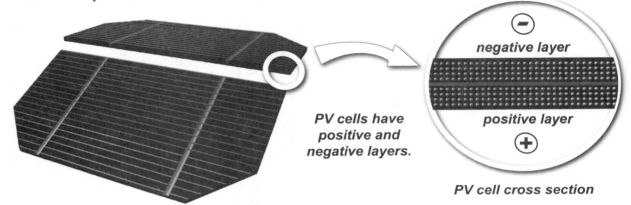

PV cells have positive and negative layers.

negative layer

positive layer

PV cell cross section

To see how solar cells work, we need to know more about the nature of light. We also need to understand some basic principles of electricity.

Photons

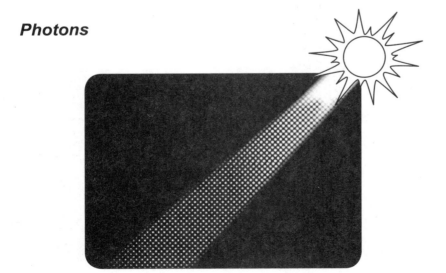

Light acts like particles called photons.

Besides acting like waves, light also behaves like a stream of tiny chunks, or particles of energy. These particles are called ***photons***.

Photons are an unusual kind of particle because they don't seem to have any weight or mass.

They also don't have any electric charge.

Electrons

Even though atoms are incredibly tiny, they aren't the smallest bits of matter. If we could look inside atoms we'd see even tinier particles. The center of the atom is called the **nucleus**. Spinning around the nucleus are particles of electricity called **electrons**.

Opposite electrical charges attract

Electrons have a negative charge. The nucleus has positively charged particles called **protons**. Opposite electrical charges attract, and pull toward each other.

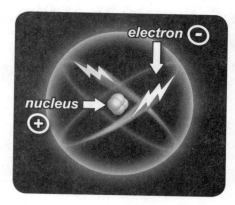

Inside an atom, electrons orbit the nucleus.

This attraction keeps the electrons in orbit around the nucleus. The electrons don't fall into the center of the atom because they have too much energy. The more energy an electron has, the bigger its orbit will be around the nucleus.

The Photovoltaic Effect

When light shines on a photovoltaic cell electricity is produced. The illustration below shows how this happens. As photons of light hit the cell, their energy is absorbed by some of the electrons in the atoms. If an electron absorbs enough energy, its orbit gets so big it breaks away from the nucleus. The electron is now a free, negatively charged particle.

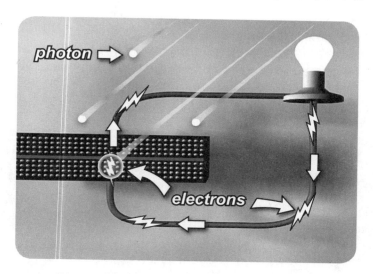

Photons release electrons from the atoms. The electrons move through the wire.

These electrons will try to return to their atoms, but the design of the cell pushes them up through the negative layer. If a wire is connected between the top and bottom layers of the cell, the electrons will flow through it, and combine with atoms in the positive layer.

This flow of negatively charged electrons is called an **electrical current**.

The process of photons releasing electrons is called the **photovoltaic effect**.

Electrical current is like the current of water in a stream, or water moving through a hose. It is a source of energy: the energy carried by the moving charged particles. In wire, these charged particles are negatively charged electrons, but positively charged protons can also carry electrical energy.

NOTE: "How a Solar Cell Works" animation viewable online at: "http://www.solarschoolhouse.org

PV Cells and PV Modules

Photovoltaic (PV) cells come in different sizes. They can be smaller than a quarter of an inch across, and bigger than five inches across. Bigger cells produce more power, but even large cells usually produce less than 3 watts. That's not enough energy to power most household appliances.

For more power, several cells are connected together in weather tight packages called **photovoltaic modules**. Photovoltaic modules are also called **solar panels** or PV modules.

Each photovoltaic cell produces a small amount of power.

To increase power, cells are grouped into photovoltaic modules (also called solar panels).

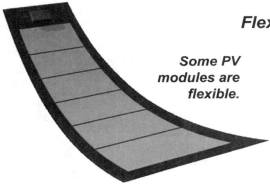

Flexible modules

Some PV modules are flexible.

There are different kinds of photovoltaic modules. Most are made with hard, crystalline silicon. Some are flexible however, and can be rolled out and glued onto metal roofs.

Solar arrays

Even large solar panels don't produce a huge amount of electric power.

To supply electricity for an entire house, many solar panels are connected together in a large group called a **solar array** (or **photovoltaic array**).

PV modules can be connected together in a solar array.

How to Get the Most Electricity from Solar Panels

Daily sun angles

Remember: more energy is absorbed when light strikes at a 90 degree angle. PV modules generate the most electricity when facing the sun directly.

This means that a solar panel placed flat on the ground will produce different amounts of power thoughout the day.

It will produce more electricity at noon when the sun is most directly overhead, and less in the morning and afternoon when the sun is lower in the sky.

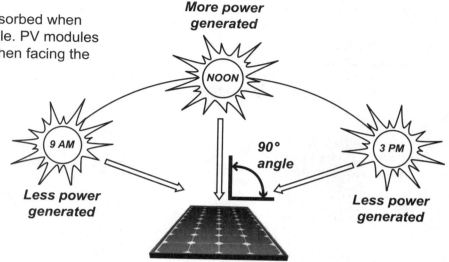

A 90 degree angle produces the most electricity.

Tilt angles

North of the equator, a solar panel flat on the ground would not face the sun directly. Even at noon, it would be tilted slightly away.

The farther north you are, the greater this tilt will be.

To correct for this, the solar panel is angled up toward the south to face the sun.

This tilt angle is equal to the **latitude**, a number which measures the distance a place is from the equator.

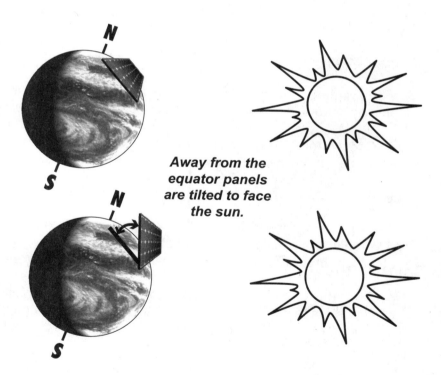

Away from the equator panels are tilted to face the sun.

Shadows

Be sure to keep PV modules out of the shade, and in direct sunlight. This is most important in the the middle of the day when the sun supplies the most energy. Even a shadow the size of person's hand greatly decreases the amount of power a panel produces.

Basic Electrical Circuits

Now we know how solar cells work, and can start using them to power electrical devices. To do this, we need to create an **electrical circuit**. A circuit is a closed path for electrons to follow.

Elements of electrical circuits

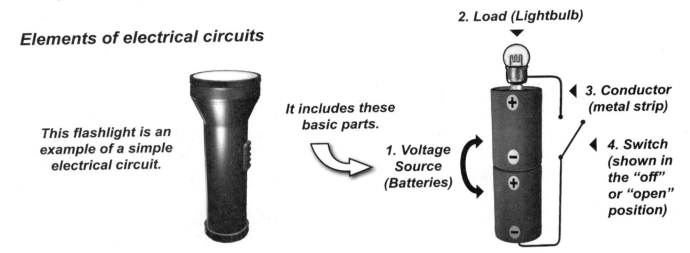

2. Load (Lightbulb)

3. Conductor (metal strip)

4. Switch (shown in the "off" or "open" position)

This flashlight is an example of a simple electrical circuit.

It includes these basic parts.

1. Voltage Source (Batteries)

1. **A voltage source** is anything that supplies electrical force. Electrical force (measured in **volts**) is what pushes electrons through the circuit. In the flashlight the batteries are the voltage source. These batteries produce about 1.5 volts of pressure. Car batteries produce about 12 volts, and the outlets in your house supply 120 volts of electrical pressure. Voltage sources have positive and negative ends. The flashlight curcuit starts at the negative end, and finishes at the positive end.

2. **A load** is anything that uses electricity. The lightbulb in the flashlight is the load. Things like electric motors, microwave ovens, and computers are other kinds of loads.

3. **Conductors** are materials that carry electricity. We know metals are good conductors of heat; they're also good conductors of electricity. The flashlight has metal conductors for the electrons to flow through.

Wires made of copper are excellent conductors. Wires are usually covered with a plastic or rubber coating. This coating acts as an **electrical insulator**, and resists the flow of electrical current.

An aligator clip makes connecting this wire easy.

4. **Switches** turn current flow on & off. They open the circuit, and make a break in the path the electrons are following. Electricity will only flow if it has an unbroken path to follow. When the switch on the side of the flashlight is 'off', it is in the open position, and the circuit is broken.

5. **Safety devices:** The flashlight doesn't have a safety device, but most circuits include a way to protect wires from overheating and causing fires. **Fuses** and **circuit breakers** are examples.

Wires heat up when electrical current flows through them. If there is too much current, they melt, or burn off their insulation. Fuses are designed to break a circuit if too much current flows.

The thin wire in this fuse melts if too much current flows.

How Electricity Works

The way electricity flows through a circuit is similar to the way water flows through pipes. Imagine a tank of water with a pipe coming out the bottom, and a valve on the pipe.

The water is heavy, and pushes down on the bottom of the tank. The water's weight pushes it through the pipe when the valve is opened.

If we put a water wheel in front of the pipe, the water current spins the wheel. The pressure pushing the water through the pipe is like electrical pressure (voltage) in circuits.

The water's weight pushes it through the pipe.
The current of water turns the wheel.

Electrical pressure (voltage)

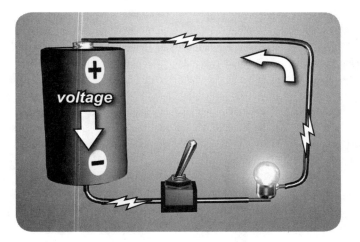

Battery voltage pushes electrons through the wire.
The current of electrons lights the bulb.

A battery is like the tank of water. One end of the battery has more electrons (negative charges). The other end has more protons (positive charges).

Opposite charges attract. The electrons push on the negative end of the battery, trying to flow through the circuit to the positive end.

Turn the switch, and this electrical force (*voltage*), pushes electrons through the wire.

Electrical current (amperage)

The current of electrons moving through the bulb makes it glow. Current is measured in *amperes* (or *amps*). An amp is a number of electrical charges moving past a point in one second. In a wire, those charges are electrons. *1 amp is about 6 quintillion electrons passing a point in a wire in one second.* That's 6,000,000,000,000,000,000 electrons a second.

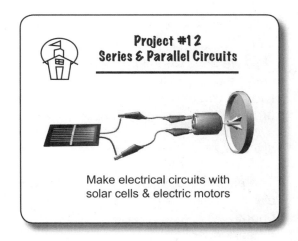

Project #12
Series & Parallel Circuits

Make electrical circuits with solar cells & electric motors

Electrical power (watts)

It takes power to turn the waterwheel, or light the lightbulb. In electrical circuits, power is measured in watts. *Watts* are units that show how fast energy is being used. Watts show how much energy is being used per second. This is the rate of energy consumption at a given moment.

Increasing Power

What if we wanted to use *more* power, to spin the waterwheel faster, for example, or make the lightbulb burn brighter?

One way to get more power is to push the water through the pipe with more pressure. To do this, we could use a taller tank.

The higher the column of water, the more it weighs, and the more pressure it exerts on the bottom of the tank.

This greater pressure pushes the water through the pipe with more force, and the more forceful current of water spins the wheel faster.

This is similar to what happens in an electric circuit when we increase the voltage.

A higher column of water pushes the current harder. The wheel spins faster.

Increasing voltage (electrical pressure)

To increase the pressure that pushes electrons through the circuit, we can connect another battery in series.

In series means we connect the batteries in a chain, attaching the positive end of one battery to the negative end of the other. This increases the voltage, but not the maximum amount of current each battery can supply. Remember:

Series wiring adds voltage.

Now we have one big battery with the combined voltage of both smaller batteries. For example: two 1.5 volt batteries connected in series (+ to -) produce 3 volts of electrical pressure.

1.5 volts + 1.5 volts = 3 volts

The pressure pushing the current through the circuit is twice as great, and the bulb will be brighter.

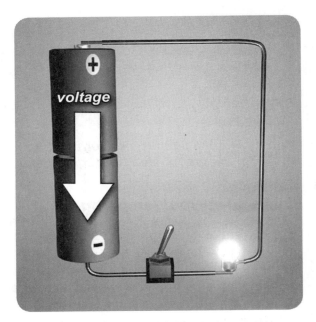

The combined voltage pushes the current harder. The bulb is brighter.

We have increased the power (watts) supplied to the lightbulb by adding the voltages of the two batteries. Sometimes, however, we need to increase the power, and keep the voltage the same. We can do this by connecting the batteries in parallel.

Increasing amperage (electrical current)

Many devices run at the same voltage, but different power levels. Most lights in your house use 120 volts, but some burn brighter than others. For example: a 100 watt bulb is much brighter than a 25 watt bulb.

25 watt bulb   100 watt bulb

The bigger bulb draws more current. More electrons per second are moving through it.

A large bulb may quickly use all the current a single battery can provide. Batteries only provide current for limited amount of time before they "run out". To draw more current, for a longer time, a second battery is connected in parallel.

In parallel means the postive ends of the batteries are connected to each other, and the negative ends are too. Now the current has two paths to follow through the batteries.

Once they're connected in parallel, each battery only needs to supply half of the current drawn by the lightbulb.

Parallel wiring

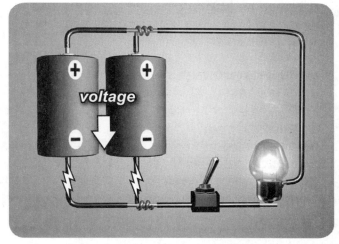

The maximum current available from the batteries is added together. Voltage stays the same.

The voltage stays the same as it is for one battery, but the maximum amount of current available from each battery is added together. Remember:

Parallel adds amps; volts stay the same.

The Power Formula

Units of power (watts) measure the amount of energy produced or used per second. We've seen how to get more power in two ways: by increasing current (parallel wiring), and by increasing voltage (series wiring). This works because power is the product of voltage times amperage.

Watts = volts x amps (or volts = watts ÷ amps, or amps = watts ÷ volts)

This is the "*power formula*," and it lets us get the same amount of power at different voltages.

For example: We have *120 volt circuits* in our homes. At 120 volts, it takes 0.5 amps to power a 60 watt lightbulb. *120 volts x 0.5 amps = 60 watts.*

We have *12 volt circuits* in our cars. Some headlights use 60 watts. At 12 volts, it takes 5 amps to power a 60 watt headlight. *12 volts x 5 amps = 60 watts.*

Using Solar Electricity

We can use photovoltaic cells as a voltage supply instead of batteries. The principles are the same, except PV cells only supply power when light shines on them.

PV cells can be wired in series (+ to -) to increase voltage. This is important because each cell only supplies about 0.5 volt. Many electrical appliances need at least 12 volts, and the devices we use in our homes need 120 volts. This is one reason why solar panels are made with several individual cells wired in series: to increase their voltage. Many solar panels supply 12 volts; some supply 24 volts or more.

There are many ways to use solar electricity in our homes. Let's start with the simplest.

PV direct systems

We can attach PV cells directly to the equipment we want to power. A common example is a solar powered calculator. The calculator has a built in solar panel. This is called a **PV direct system**. The solar panel is connected directly to the load. Solar powered calculators need very little electricity, and can even run on indoor light. Many PV direct systems need more power, and only work in direct sunlight.

Solar powered calculator

To have power when the sun isn't shining, one or more batteries are added to the circuit. This is called a **battery backup system**.

Battery backup systems

Battery backup systems store energy during the day to use at night. The solar panel is connected to a battery, and charges it during the day. At night the battery powers the load.

Battery backup systems charge batteries during the day...

...and the batteries power the load at night.

Large battery backup systems use many photovoltaic modules and several batteries. They can power wilderness cabins, sailboats and even large homes. Battery backup systems need a device called a **charge controller** to make sure the batteries are charged correctly.

Types of Electricity

If we want to power our houses with solar electricity, there's something else we need to know. The type of electricity we get from solar panels is not the same type of electricity supplied to our homes. These are two different kinds of electricity: direct current (or DC) electricity and alternating current (or AC) electricity.

Direct Current

All of the circuits we've looked at so far use *direct current (DC) electricity*. Direct current travels through a wire in only one direction: from negative to positive. Batteries and photovoltaic modules supply DC electricity. Most devices in your home run on a different type of electricity: alternating current.

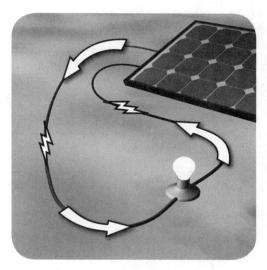

DC electricity flows in only one direction: from negative to positive.

Alternating current

Alternating current (AC) electricity is a back-and-forth movement of electrons. First the current flows in one direction, and then it changes direction, and flows the other way. The direction of current flow *alternates* back-and-forth 60 times a second. This is the type of electricity supplied to homes and businesses by electric utility companies.

AC electricity flows in one direction...

...then "alternates" and flows the other way.

Utitlity companies produce electricity with large generators. These generators run on different sources of energy including fossil fuels, hydropower and nuclear energy. The electricity is then sent through power lines as high voltage alternating current. This system of generators and power lines is called the *utility grid*.

A meter measures how much electricity we use.

Before it enters our homes, the electricity passes through an *electric meter*, which measures how much electricity we use.

Inverters

To run the devices in our homes on the direct current supplied by solar panels, we need to turn it into alternating current. The device that does this is called an *inverter*.

Inverters change the DC electricity from batteries and solar panels into the AC electricity used in our homes. They also change the voltage.

Solar arrays are often wired to supply 12, 24 or 48 volts of direct current. The inverter turns this low voltage DC electricity into the 120 volt alternating current used by household lights, TVs and other appliances.

Inverters change DC electricity into AC electricity.

Utility Intertie Systems

There's another way to make electricity during the day, and have it available at night. It's called a *utility intertie system* (also called a *gridtie system*). Gridtie systems don't need batteries. They use a special inverter that can pump electricity from the solar panels into the utility grid.

During the day the solar array pumps electricity through the inverter into the grid, and the electric meter turns backwards. At night, or when using more electricity than the solar array produces, electricity flows from the utility grid, and the meter turns forward.

During the day electricity flows through the inverter into the grid.

At night electricity flows from the utility grid into the house.

Net Metering

Many utility companies give credit for the electricity supplied to the grid by the solar array. The value of the electricity pumped into the grid is subtracted from the cost of the electricity taken out. This is called *net metering*.

Solar History

In 1953, the Bell telephone system had a problem. Traditional dry cell batteries that worked fine in mild climates degraded too rapidly in the tropics and ceased to work when needed. The company asked its famous research arm, Bell Laboratories, to explore other freestanding sources of electricity. It assigned the task to Daryl Chapin. Chapin tested wind machines, thermoelectric generators, and steam engines. He also suggested that the investigation include solar cells, and his supervisor approved the idea.

Chapin soon discovered that selenium solar cells, the only type on the market, produced too little power, a mere five watts per square meter, and converted less than 0.5 percent of the incoming sunlight into electricity. Word of Chapin's problems came to the attention of another Bell researcher, Gerald Pearson. This was not strange, since Pearson and Chapin had been friends for years. They had attended the same university, and Pearson had even spent time on Chapin's tulip farm.

At the time, Pearson was engaged in pioneering semiconductor research with Calvin Fuller. They took silicon solid-state devices from their experimental stage to commercialization. Fuller, a chemist, had discovered how to control the introduction of the impurities necessary to transform silicon from a poor to a superior conductor of electricity.

The first advertisement for the Bell solar cell, from the August 1954 issue of National Geographic.

P-N Junction

Fuller provided Pearson with a piece of silicon containing a small amount of gallium. The introduction of gallium made it positively charged. Pearson then dipped the gallium-rich silicon into a hot lithium bath, according to Fuller's instructions. Where the lithium penetrated, an area of poorly bound electrons was created, and it became negatively charged. A permanent electrical force developed where the positive and negative silicon meet. This is the P-N junction, the core of any semiconductor device.

The P-N junction is like a dry riverbed, which has an incline that provides the means for flow, should it fill with water. The P-N junction will push electrons in an orderly fashion, commonly called electrical current, when some type of energy hits those loosely bound electrons nearby with enough power to tear them away from their atomic glue. Shining lamplight onto the lithiumgallium doped silicon provided the necessary energy, and Pearson's ammeter recorded a significant electron flow. To Pearson's surprise, he had made a solar cell superior to any other available at the time.

Pearson, Chapin, & Fuller principal developers of the silicon solar cell

Silicon Is the Answer

Hearing of his colleague's poor results with selenium, Pearson went directly to Chapin's office to advise him not to waste another moment on selenium, and to start working on silicon. Chapin's tests on the new material proved Pearson right. Exposing Pearson's silicon solar cell to strong sunlight, Chapin found that it performed significantly better than the selenium—it was five times more efficient.

Theoretical calculations brought even more encouraging news. An ideal silicon solar cell, Chapin figured, could use 23 percent of the incoming solar energy to produce electricity. But building a silicon solar cell that would convert around 6 percent of sunlight into electricity would satisfy Chapin and rank as a viable energy source. His colleagues concurred and all his work focused on this goal.

Try as he might, though, Chapin could not improve on what Pearson had accomplished. "The biggest problem," Chapin reported, "appears to be making electrical contact to the silicon." Not being able to solder the leads right to the cell forced Chapin to electroplate a portion of the negative and positive silicon layers to tap into the electricity generated by the cell. Unfortunately, no metal plate would adhere well, presenting a seemingly insurmountable obstacle to grabbing more of the electricity generated.

Moving the Junction

Chapin also had to cope with the inherent instability of the lithium-bathed silicon, which moved deep into the cell at room temperatures. This caused the location of the P-N junction, the core of any photovoltaic device, to leave its original location at the surface, making it more difficult for light to penetrate the junction, where all photovoltaic activity occurs.

Then, an inspired guess changed Chapin's tack. He correctly hypothesized, "It appears necessary to make our P-N junction very next to the surface so that nearly all the photons are effective." He turned to Calvin Fuller for advice on creating a solar cell that would permanently fix the P-N junction at the top of the cell.

Coincidentally, Fuller had done just that two years earlier while trying to make a transistor. He then replicated his prior work to satisfy his colleague's need. Instead of doping the cell with lithium, the chemist vaporized a small amount of phosphorous onto the otherwise positive silicon. The new concoction almost doubled previous performance records.

Solar Cell vs. Atomic Battery

Still, the lingering failure to obtain good contacts frustrated Chapin from reaching the 6 percent efficiency goal he was aiming for. While Chapin's work reached an impasse, arch rival RCA announced that its scientists had come up with a nuclear-powered silicon cell, dubbed the atomic battery. Its development coincided with the U.S Atoms for Peace program, which promoted the use of nuclear energy throughout the world.

Calvin Fuller placing arsenic-laced silicon into a quartz-tube furnace.

Instead of photons supplied by the sun, the atomic battery ran on those emitted from Strontium 90, one of the deadliest nuclear residues. To showcase the new invention, RCA decided to put on a dramatic presentation in New York City. David Sarnoff, founder and president of RCA, who had initially gained fame as the telegraph operator who tapped out the announcement to the world that the Titanic had sunk, hit the keys of an old-fashioned telegraph powered by the atomic battery to send the message, "Atoms for Peace." The atomic battery, according to RCA, would one day power homes, cars, and locomotives with radioactive waste— Strontium 90—produced by nuclear reactors.

What its public relations people failed to mention, however, was why the Venetian blinds had to be closed during Sarnoff's demonstration. Years later, one of the lead scientists involved in the project came clean: If the silicon device had been exposed to the sun's rays, solar energy would have overpowered the contribution of the Strontium 90. Had the nuclear element been turned off, the battery would have continued to work on the solar energy streaming through the window.

The director of RCA Laboratories did not mince words when he ordered his scientific staff to go along with the deception, telling them, "Who cares about solar energy? Look, what we have is this radioactive waste converter. That's the big thing that's going to catch the attention of the public, the press, the scientific community."

The director had gauged the media well. The New York Times, for example, called Sarnoff's demonstration "prophetic." It predicted that electricity from the atomic battery would allow "hearing aids and wrist watches [to] run continuously for the whole of a man's useful life."

Cells with a Future

RCA's success stirred management at Bell Laboratories to pressure the solar investigators to hurry up and produce something newsworthy as well. Luckily for them, Fuller had busied himself in his lab to discover an entirely new way to make more efficient solar cells. He began with silicon cut into long, narrow strips modeled after Chapin's best performing cells. That's where the similarity ended.

Instead of adding gallium to the pure silicon and producing positive silicon, Fuller introduced a minute amount of arsenic to to make the starting material negative. Then he placed the arsenic-doped silicon into a furnace to coat it with a layer of boron. The controlled introduction of an ultrathin layer of boron gave the cell a P-N junction extremely close to the surface. The Bell team had no trouble in making good electrical contacts to the boron-arsenic silicon cells, resolving the main obstacle in extracting electricity when exposing them to sunlight.

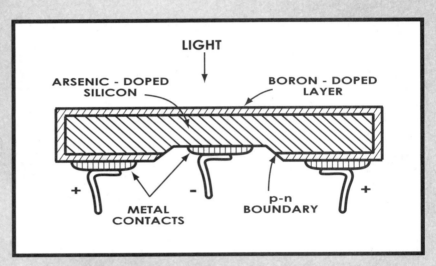

Cross-section diagram of the first Bell power cell doped with boron and arsenic.

All cells built according to Fuller's new method did much better than previously. One, however, outperformed the rest, reaching the efficiency goal Chapin had set. The best-performing cell seemed to have the ideal width for peak performance. Bell scientists built cells to the same dimensions as that bestperforming cell.

Chapin then confidently referred to these as "photocells intended to be primary power sources." Assured of success, the Bell solar team began putting together modules to publicly demonstrate this major breakthrough. On April 25, 1954, proud Bell executives held a press conference where they impressed the media with Bell solar cells powering a radio transmitter, broadcasting voice and music. One journalist thought it important for the public to know that "linked together electrically, the Bell solar cells deliver power from the sun at the rate of fifty watts per square yard while the atomic cell announced recently by the RCA Corporation merely delivers a millionth of a watt" over the same area. U.S. News & World Report believed one day such silicon strips "may provide more power than all the world's coal, oil, and uranium."

Harnessing the Sun

The New York Times probably best summed up what Chapin, Fuller, and Pearson had accomplished. On page one of its April 26, 1954 issue, it stated that the construction of the first PV module to generate useful amounts of electricity marks "the beginning of a new era, leading eventually to the realization of one of mankind's most cherished dreams—the harnessing of the almost limitless energy of the sun for the uses of civilization."

Just think: fifty years ago the world had less than a watt of solar cells capable of running electrical equipment. Today, fifty years later, a billion watts of solar-electric modules are in use around the world.

They run satellites; ensure the safe passage of ships and trains; bring water, electricity, and telephone service to many who had done without; and supply clean energy to those already connected to the grid. We hope that the next fifty years will see solar cells on rooftops throughout the world, fulfilling the expectation triggered by the pioneering work of Chapin, Fuller, and Pearson.

John Perlin

Review Questions

1. The device that changes light into electricity is called a
_____ cell.

2. Most solar modules are made of
A. Silicon
B. The most common element in the Earth's crust
C. A semiconductor material
D. All of the above

3. Light acts like waves, and like
A. Electrons
B. Protons
C. Particles

4. Individual packets of light energy are called _____.

5. The center of an atom is called the _____.

6. The center of an atom is surrounded by negatively-charged particles called
_____.

7. A group of photovoltaic modules connected together is called a:
A. Solar array
B. Solar system
C. Solar assembly
D. All of the above

8. The force, or pressure, pushing electrical charges through a wire is called:
A. Current
B. Voltage
C. Wattage

9. Electrons flowing through a wire are called:
A. Current
B. Volts
C. Watts

9. Electrical current is measured in _____.

10. To increase voltage connect batteries:
A. In series (+ to -, + to -)
B. In parallel (+ to +, - to -)
C. With the power formula

11. The units of power that measure how fast electricity is generated or used:
A. Current
B. Volts
C. Watts

12. Watts equals _____ times _____.

13. A 6 volt bicycle light draws half of an amp. How many watts is it using?

14. A 36 watt headlight is running at 12 volts. How much current is it drawing?

15. Batteries and solar modules provide _____ electricity.

16. The electric utility provides _____ electricity.

17. The device which feeds electricity from solar panels into the utility grid:
_____.

18. A system connecting a solar array with the utility grid is called a:
_____ system.

19. The first solar cell that could produce enough electricity for useful purposes was made public in what year?
a. 1954
b. 1876
c. 1976

7 System Sizing

How Much Energy Do You Need?

Solar energy systems can heat and cool buildings, cook food, heat water and make electricity. How big do these systems need to be? That depends mainly on 3 things:

1. Where you live
2. The size & lifestyle of your family
3. How efficiently you use energy

The size and location of our family makes a big difference in the size of our systems. A house in the arctic needs more south-facing windows than the same house in the desert. A larger family needs a bigger solar hot water system. We can't do too much about family size and location, but there are many things we can do to use energy more efficiently.

Using Energy Efficiently

Using energy efficiently means doing the same job with less energy. Super-efficient washing machines, for example, use much less electricity and water. By using energy efficiently we can meet our needs with smaller, less expensive solar energy systems.

Over half of home energy is used to heat and cool buildings, and to heat water (U.S. Department of Energy). In previous chapters we covered many ways to do these things with sunlight. Now we'll see how to do them more efficiently. Then we'll focus on energy efficiency and solar electricity.

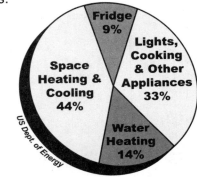

After discussing more efficient ways to use electricity, we'll see how to measure how much electricity we consume. This information is used to find out how many solar modules we need to power our home.

Average U.S.A. home energy use

Heating, Cooling and Hot Water

Passive solar homes sometimes need fossil fuel-powered heaters and air conditioners when the weather is very hot or cold. Heaters can be used less if heating vents are closed in unused rooms, curtains are drawn after sunset, and thermostats set to 55°F at bedtime. Air conditioners can be used less if curtains are closed on summer days, and thermostats set to 78 degrees and above.

There are many inexpensive ways to conserve the energy used to heat water too. The easiest is to use less hot water. Low flow showerheads use less water, and as a result, less energy is needed to heat the water.

Washing clothes with cold water helps too. The U.S. Department of Energy estimates that about 80% to 85% of the energy used for washing clothes goes to heating the water.

Low flow showerheads save energy & water.

Fixing leaky hot water faucets and installing water-efficent faucet heads also saves energy inexpensively. So does insulating water heaters and hot water pipes.

Lighting, Cooking and Appliances

The rest of household energy goes to lighting, cooking and appliances. Lighting is one of the easiest areas to save energy.

Standard (incandescent) lightbulbs are very wasteful. Only about 10% of the energy they use is given out as light, according to the California Energy Commission. The other 90% of the energy just heats up the lightbulb. Fortunately, there are other kinds of lightbulbs we can use.

Compact Fluorescents

Compact Fluorescent Lamps, or CFL's, use much less electricity, and give the same amount of light. Over 80% of the energy they use is given out as light.

CFL's cost more, but last up to 10 times longer than regular bulbs. They are also 3 to 4 times more efficient at producing light. A 15 watt CFL can produce the same amount of light as a 60 watt incandescent bulb. They save money in the long run.

Compact Fluorescent Lamps

Which appliances should run on solar power?

Most modern homes have a variety of household appliances like toasters, TV's and microwave ovens. All of these appliances can be powered by the solar electricity, but some of them should run on other fuels. In general, large appliances used for heating and cooking should *not* run on solar electricity.

Clothes dryers and electric stoves for example, would need very large and expensive solar arrays. It's better to use a clothesline when possible, and have a gas-powered clothes dryer for backup.

If it's not possible to use a solar oven, a gas stove is better than an electric stove running on solar panels.

When using solar electricity, It's best to use the most energy efficient appliances, ones that can be powered by the smallest possible photovoltaic system. This is especially true with refrigerators.

Electric stoves and clothes dryers should not run on solar power.

Refrigerators

Refrigerators are one of the biggest energy hogs in the home. They often need more electricity than any other appliance, except air conditioners and electric water heaters. Newer models are much more efficient. In fact, many of today's refrigerators use a fraction of the electricity used by a 15 year old model.

This is important because many referigerators last over 20 years. When using solar electricity, It's usually cheaper in the long run to buy a new, energy efficient fridge. The cost of a new fridge is much less than the cost of the extra PV modules needed to power an old, ineffecent model.

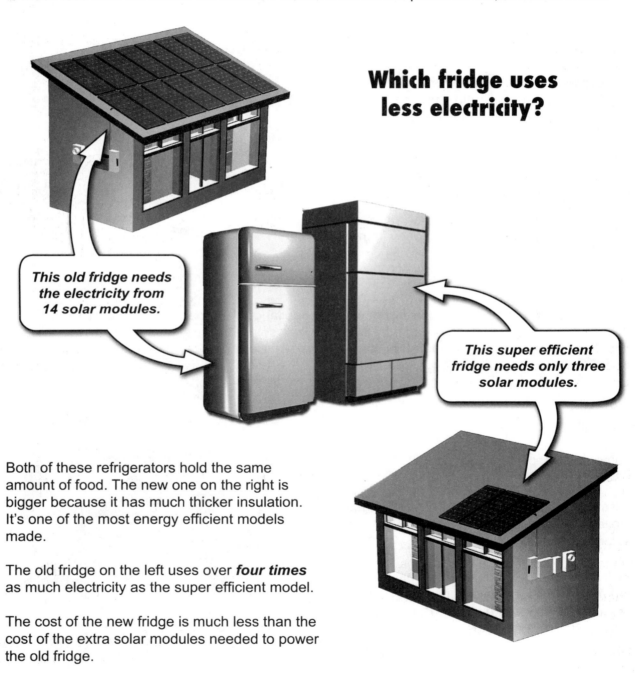

Which fridge uses less electricity?

This old fridge needs the electricity from 14 solar modules.

This super efficient fridge needs only three solar modules.

Both of these refrigerators hold the same amount of food. The new one on the right is bigger because it has much thicker insulation. It's one of the most energy efficient models made.

The old fridge on the left uses over **four times** as much electricity as the super efficient model.

The cost of the new fridge is much less than the cost of the extra solar modules needed to power the old fridge.

Energy Guide Label

When shopping for an energy efficient fridge, or other appliance, imagine two price tags. The first is the purchase price. The second price tag is the cost of running the appliance over its lifetime. You pay on that second price tag every month with your utility bill.

If you use solar electricity, the second price tag is the cost of the photovoltaic equipment needed to power the appliance.

To get an idea of how much energy a new appliance will use, look at the Energy Guide Label posted on it. The **Energy Guide Label** shows about how much electricity an appliance will use per year, and compares it to similar appliances.

Phantom Loads

Phantom loads are appliances that use electricity even when switched "off"". Things like TV's, VCR's, garage door openers, and any device that can be turned on by a remote control are phantom loads. They're always "listening" to receive the signal from the remote.

Devices with an electric clock, like a microwave oven or a VCR, also use a small amount of electrcity all the time.

VCR's and other phantom loads use electricity even when turned "off."

Phantom Loads may only use a few extra watts, but this energy adds up, and can require extra PV modules. By plugging them into switched outlets or power strips, phantom loads can be completely turned off when not in use.

Vampires

Some small appliances, like telephone answering machines, electric toothbrushes and cordless phones, have little transformer cubes at the end of their power cords.

These are known in the electric industry as **vampires** becuase they "suck" electricity even when the device they're powering is "off."

They're also very ineffecent. For every dime of energy they use, 6 to 8 cents is wasted as heat. That's why they're always warm. If possible "vampires" should be unplugged, or attached to power strips and switched off, when not in use.

Vampires suck energy.

Phantom loads & vampires connected to powerstrips can be turned "off."

Energy Audits

Now that we've seen several ways to conserve electricity, let's find out how much we actually use in our homes. One way to do this is to perform an electric energy audit.

An **energy audit** measures how much energy is used in a building, paying special attention to how energy is wasted. There are different kinds of energy audits. Some look at all forms of energy use. Others focus on a single type of energy, like electricity.

An electric energy audit is a very important first step before installing a photovoltaic system, because it tells us how big a system we'll need. We can identify which loads use the most electricity, and which can be replaced with more efficient equipment. Before we begin an electric energy audit, we'll have to know how electricity is measured.

Measuring Electricity Use

There are two ways to measure electricity use. We can measure **how fast** a device uses electricity, and we can measure **how much** electricity it uses over a period of time.

So far we've been measuring how fast a device uses electricity. A 100 watt lightbulb, for example, uses electricity twice as fast as a 50 watt bulb. It uses twice as much energy per second as a 50 watt bulb.

Rate of Energy Use

This can also be called the **rate of energy use**. The higher an electric device's rate of energy use, the more electricity it uses per second.

Remember that watts is a measurement of power. Power is just another way of saying "rate of energy use." A watt is a measurement of how much electrical energy is being used per second.

Watts measure the speed at which electricity is converted into other forms of energy, like light and heat.

A 100 watt bulb uses electricity twice as fast as a 50 watt bulb.

"Watts" is like "miles per hour." Both show how fast something is happening. Both measure rate or speed. But remember: there's no such thing as "watts per hour". Watts is already a measurement of speed. Saying "watts per hour" is like saying "miles per hour per hour."

Watts and Kilowatts

Different loads consume energy at different speeds. A small TV, for example, may use 100 watts. An electric heater can use over 1,000 watts. A thousand watts is also called a **kilowatt**, (**or KW**)

1,000 watts = 1 kilowatt

The more watts a device uses, the more electrical energy it consumes for every second it's on. This is often called the **wattage** of the device, whether it's 1 watt or 10 kilowatts.

Total energy used

Now we'll measure the total amount of energy used by an appliance over a period of time, like an hour, a day, or a month, or a year. To do this we need to know the wattage of the appliance, and how many total hours we've used it. Multipy these two numbers, and you have the total energy consumed by the appliance. The equation for energy used is:

Energy Used = Power x Time

It's often abbreviated like this: E = P x T. Remember: power (watts) is the rate of energy use.

Watt-Hours and Kilowatt Hours

The units of the equation are:

Energy Used (in watt-hours) = Power (in watts) x Time (in hours)

For example, if an electric heater uses 1,000 watts (1 kilowatt) of electricity, and we have it on for 1 hour, we'll use 1,000 watt-hours (1 kilowatt-hour) of electricity.

1,000 watts x 1 hour = 1,000 watt-hours

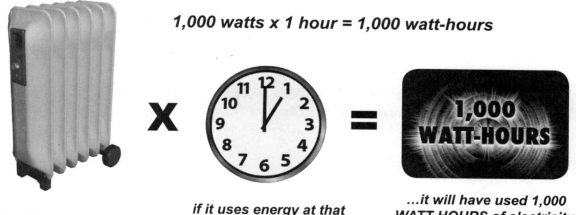

This heater uses electricity at a rate of 1,000 Watts...

if it uses energy at that rate for 1 hour...

...it will have used 1,000 WATT-HOURS of electricity.

The term "watt-hours" may seem confusing, since we just said there's no such thing as "watts per hour." Watt-hours are different. **Watt-hours (or WH)** are an **amount** of energy, not a speed, or rate of energy use. Watt-hours are like miles traveled, and watts are like miles per hour.

A **kilowatt-hour** is equal to 1,000 watt-hours. It's often abbreviated as: KWH or kWh.

1,000 watts-hours = 1 kilowatt-hour (KWH)

Auditing Loads

Now that we know how to measure electricity, we can begin the electric energy audit. Start by figuring out how much electricity is used by every device in the house each week. Then divide that figure by 7 to get a daily total.

This is the first step in finding out how many solar panels we'll need to supply our electricity.

First find the wattage of each load. The wattage is usually printed somewhere on the device. Often it's on the back or bottom of an appliance, or on its "nameplate".

Sometimes only the amperage and voltage are shown. We can use the power formula to find the wattage of the appliance.

watts = volts x amps

Multiplying the voltage times the amperage will give us the wattage of the appliance.

For example, the nameplate at the right is from an appliance that uses 1 amp at 120 volts. 120 volts is typical for a household circuit.

120 volts X 1 amp = 120 watts

Here are some sample wattages:

WAFFLEWIZARD INC.
Toastown, Mo. U.S.A.
120v 1200W 60Hz.
MODEL 345
HOUSEHOLD TYPE

Made in USA
LIsted
Oven Broiler 422B

Look for the wattage on the appliance nameplate.

Model No.	**CTZ-1651B**	
Serial No.	MR1149872	
Power Rating **120V 60HZ**		Max Amps **1.0**
Manufactured	**MAY 1998**	

Sometimes all that's listed is voltage and amperage.

POWER USED BY APPLIANCES (IN WATTS)			
CD player	35	Lights:	
Clock radio	10	Incandescent	100
Coffee maker	800-1200	CFL (100 watt equivalent)	30
Clothes washer	350-500	Microwave oven	750-1100
Clothes dryer	1800-5000	Refrigerator (hours per day)	
Computer		Old 16 cubic foot (13 hours)	475
PC - awake / asleep	120 / 30	New 16 cu. ft. (7 hrs)	145
Monitor - awake / asleep	150 / 30	TV (color) 19"	110
Laptop	50	25"	150
Dishwasher	1200-2400	Toaster	800-1400
Electric blanket	60-100	VCR/DVD player	20-40
Fan-Ceiling	50-175	Vacuum cleaner	1000-1440
Hair dryer	1200-1875	Washer (standard, .5 hr per load)	600
Heater (portable)	750-1500	Washer (super-efficient, .5 hr per load)	300
Clothes Iron	1000-1800	Water heater (40 gallon)	4500-5500

Hours of Use

Once you know how quickly each device consumes electricity (its wattage) you need to find out how many hours each day you use it. You may have to estimate, or give it your best guess. Some appliances like refrigerators only run part of the time. Others, like washing machines, are not used everyday. You can list this information in a chart like the one below.

Electric Device	Watts	X	Hours used per day	X	Days used per week	÷	7	=	Average watt-hours per day
Fridge	145	X	7 hours	X	7 days	÷	7	=	1,015 WH
Washing Machine	500	X	0.5 hours	X	4 days	÷	7	=	143 WH
Fluorescent light	30	X	3 hours	X	7 days	÷	7	=	90 WH
CD player	35	X	3 hours	X	5 days	÷	7	=	75 WH

Total average watt-hours used per day = 3,170 WH

Electric Bills

There are other ways to find out how much electricity you use on average each day. The easiest is with your electric bill. Utility companies charge you for electricity by the kilowatt-hour (or KWH). Every month the utility company sends a bill charging a certain amout for each kilowatt-hour used.

The bill below shows average daily KWH consumption this month, last month and this month last year. It also has a graph that shows monthly KWH usage over the last year.

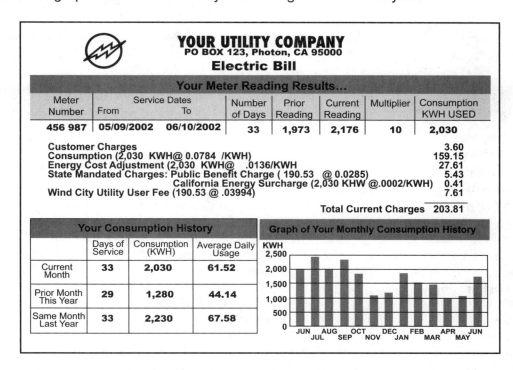

The utility company knows how many KWH you've used by looking at (or "reading") your electric meter. Electric meters give us a third way to measure energy use.

Electric meters

Your electric meter is on the outside of the house, where the power lines are attached to the building. It measures energy use in two ways. It shows **how fast** you're using energy right now, and it shows **how much** total energy you've used.

You can read your meter at the same time each day to see how much electricity you've used. If you shut off all loads, it will tell you if there are any phantom loads. If you have only one load on, the meter will show how many watts that load uses.

The meter has two types of dials on the front:

1. A set of small dials facing you
2. One large dial facing up.

As electricity flows through the meter into the building, it causes these dials to turn. The top set of small dials shows how many total kilowatt-hours have been used since the meter was installed. They turn so slowly it's hard to tell they're moving.

The large dial in the middle measures a smaller amount of electricity, and moves more quickly. The speed at which it turns is an indication of how fast your household is using electricity. The faster it turns, the faster you're using electricity. The faster it turns, the more watts you're using.

Electric meters show HOW MUCH electricity you have used over time...

...and HOW FAST you're using electricity right now!

The top set of dials shows how much electricity you've used over time.

The speed of the big dial shows how fast you're using electricity right now.

The small dials show place values of the number of kilowatt-hours. The dial farthest to the right shows the ones; the next position to the left is the tens, then the hundreds, thousands, and finally ten-thousands of kilowatt-hours.

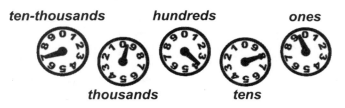

Electric meters and speedometers

An electric meter is a little like a speedometer in a car. Both show speed (rate) and totals.

The speedometer needle shows how fast the car is moving in miles per hour. The speed of the big dial in the electric meter shows how fast electricity is being used, in energy per second (watts). The faster the dial spins, the more energy per second is being used.

The odometer in a car shows how far you've traveled, in miles. The small dials of an electric meter show how much electricity you've used, in kilowatt-hours.

Electric meter (top view)

The big dial shows how fast you're using electricity, in energy per second (watts).

The small dials show how many total killowatt-hours you've used.

Speedometer

A speedometer needle shows how fast you're going, in miles per hour.

The odometer shows how many total miles you've traveled.

Projects #10   Read Your Electric Meter

It's no mystery! Your electric meter can be easily read if you know some basic principles.

Read your meter at the same time each day to see how much electricity you've used.

Array sizing

Now that we know how many kilowatt-hours per day we use, we can estimate how many solar panels will produce that much electricity. To do this we need to know two things:

1. How much power each solar panel produces in "peak sun" conditions.
2. How many hours of "peak sun' we have at our home daily.

Peak Sun

Peak sun (or "full sun equivalent") is the brightest the sun ever gets at any one instant, anywhere on Earth. It's about equal to the sunlight falling on the equator at noon on a clear day. Peak sun is equal to 1 kilowatt per square meter. Although equal to kilowatts, this is NOT electricity. This power comes as radiant energy. We can think of peak sun as "maximum solar power."

If a solar panel could turn all of that radiant energy into electricity, a 1 square meter-sized panel would produce 1 kW in peak sun. But solar panels turn about 5% to 15% of the sun's power into electricity. The most a square meter-sized panel will produce is about 150 watts.

Peak Sun = "maximum solar power"

Module manufacturers use this amount of light to test their modules. They rate their modules by how much electricity they produce under peak sun conditions.

Unless we live on the equator, we'll probably never get full peak sun conditions. The amount of sunlight at our house changes all the time too, depending on the time of day, the time of year, and how cloudy or clear the sky is.

Peak Sun Hours

Peak sun only falls on the equator for a moment at noon, then the energy decreases as the sun moves across the sky.

If that level of sunlight could last for a whole hour, a square meter of the surface would receive 1 kilowatt-hour of energy.

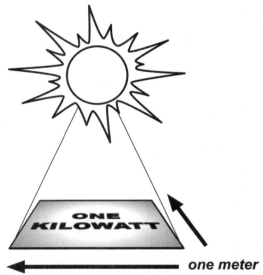

Peak sun conditions provide radiant energy at a rate of 1 KW per square meter.

This amount of solar energy is called "peak sun hours". **Peak sun hours** are just another way of saying "kilowatt-hours of radiant energy per square meter". Although we never get full peak sun conditions at our house, we can still get the **equivalent** of several peak sun hours of energy during a day. 12 hours of less than maximum solar power may add up to 5 or 6 kilowatt-hours of radiant energy. 12 hours of less than maximum solar power may equal 5 or 6 peak sun hours.

We need to find out how many hours of peak sun we get on average each day. This is the total number of peak sun hours per year divided by 365 days.

Peak Sun Hours per Day

The United States Government has measured the amount of solar energy reaching the Earth for many years. The National Renewable Energy Laboratory's (NREL) Renewable Resource Data Center provides maps showing the average number of peak sun hours a day at various places in the U.S.

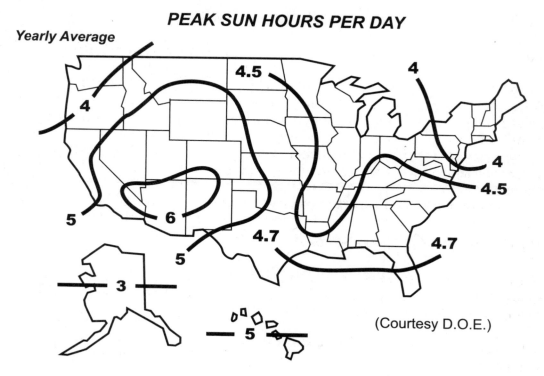

This map gives a very rough idea of how many hours of full sun equivalent per day reach areas of the United States. The amount of solar energy you receive may be very different, but we can make a rough guess. Find the line closest to your house, and record the number of average peak sun hours.

Module Output

Now we need to choose a solar panel. The manufacturers tell us how much electricity each panel produces in peak sun conditions. The module at the right is rated to produce 120 watts in peak sun.

The actual amount of energy you get from your system will be much less for many reasons. Inverters, batteries and wires lose energy. Modules aren't as efficient when they get hot. Dust on the panels can block sunlight. The actual AC output of photovoltaic modules may be closer to 70% of the manufacturers' rating.

Now we're ready to enter our data in a chart, and calculate the system size.

This module produces 120 watts in peak sun.

System Sizing Worksheet

Your energy audit will show you how many average watt-hours per day you use (line 1). Divide line 1 by a .7 to make up for inefficiencies in the system (line 2). This gives the total number of watt-hours your solar panels need to produce each day on average (line 3).

On line 4 enter the average number of peak sun hours in your region from the chart on the last page. Divide line 3 by line 4. This gives the total number of watts your solar array needs to provide at peak power (line 5). Divide by the number of watts each module produces, and you have the total number of modules you need (line 7). Round up to the nearest whole number.

Sample worksheet using data from energy audit on page 91

1.	Average Watt-hours used per day		3,170
2.	70% Efficiency correction factor	÷	.7
3.	Total daily watt-hours	=	4529
4.	Average peak sun hours per day	÷	5
5.	Solar array peak watts	=	906
6.	Module wattage rating	÷	120
7.	Number of modules in array	=	8

Sizing a solar electric system is actually more complicated than this. There are many other things to consider, like how many volts your system will run at, and whether you want a gridtie or battery backup system.

Now you know the basic principles for powering your home with the sun.

Review Questions

1. Using energy efficiently means doing the same job with _____ _____.

2. Compared to regular lightbulbs, compact fluorescent lights:
A. Are 3 to 4 times more efficient at producing light
B. Last up to 10 times longer
C. Cost more to buy, but save money in the long run
D. All of the above

3. True or False: Large appliances used for heating and cooking should not run on solar electricity.

4. Which of the following is not a phantom load:
A. VCR
B. Garage door opener
C. TV with remote control
D. None of the above

5. A_____ is a unit of measurement that shows how fast a device is generating or consuming electricity

6. True or False: Kilowatt-hours measure how much electricity has been used.

7. One kilowatt equals _____ watts.

8. Energy used = power x _____.

9. A radio draws 20 watts for two hours. How much electricity has it used?

10. An electric meter can show:
A. How much electricity you use each day
B. How fast you're using electricity right now
C. How much electricity you've used this month
D. All of the above

11. True or False: Peak Sun is the maximum power available from the Sun.

12. Peak Sun is equal to _____ per square meter.

13. Commercial solar modules convert how much of the Sun's energy into electricity?
A. about 65% to 85%
B. about 2% to 3%
C. about 5% to 15%

14. A vacuum cleaner draws 8 amps. The utility provides 120 volts. How fast does the vacuum use electricity (in watts)?

15. Your old fridge uses 5 kilowatt hours per day, and you get an average of 5 hours of Peak Sun per day. How many watts must your solar array provide at maximum power to run your refrigerator? (Assume 100% efficiency).

16. The refrigerator in Question #15 "runs" for 10 hours a day. How many amps does it draw? (House voltage = 120 volts) Round off your answer to the nearest tenth of an amp.
A. 5.7
B. 4.2
C. 500

Projects

Project #1

Cereal Box Sundial

Make a sundial using a cereal box and a stick. Watch the shadow of the stick change as the sun moves across the sky, and use the shadow to tell time.

Materials

- Empty cereal box
- Pens, pencils or crayons of at least 2 colors
- Paper
- Tape or gluestick
- Kabob stick or pencil
- Chalk
- Pushpin or small nail
- Compass

What to Do

1. Remove the liner from inside the cereal box. Draw arrows on the top, bottom and sides of the box.

2. Label one long side **"South".**

3. Poke the kabob stick through the box at an angle as shown. It helps to make 2 holes first with a pushpin or a nail.

4. Glue or tape a piece of paper on the top of the box.

5. Use a compass to find south.

6. Early in the morning, place the cereal box on the ground. Make sure the side labeled "South" points to the south.

7. Mark the points where the arrows meet the ground with chalk. Draw a triangle where the "South" arrow touches the ground. This is so you can put the box in the same place if you move it.

8. At 10 am, mark where the stick's shadow is with a pencil. Write the time below this mark.

9. Mark the shadow again at 11 am, 12 noon and 1 pm.

10. Look at your sundial and guess where the shadow will be at 2 PM. Mark where you think the shadow will be on your sundial. Use a different color for this mark.

The Next Day

1. Return the sundial to the marked position at 2 PM, align the arrows, and see if your guess for the 2 PM shadow was right.

2. Mark the real shadow and compare it with your guess.

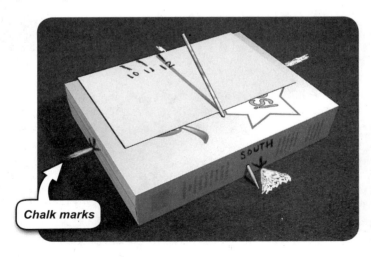

Chalk marks

Project #2

Sun Angle Tool

Make a sun angle tool, and use it to chart changes in the sun's altitude through the seasons. Use the tool to measure the shadow cast by a 4' high dowel. Then draw the measurements on graph paper to find the sun's angle in the sky. Take more measurements, and graph the changes in the sun's angle over time.

NOTE: This project uses a saw and drill, and should be done with the help of an adult!

Materials
- 1" x 6" pine board
- 3/8" dowel
- Drill and 3/8" drillbit
- Saw
- Pencil and permanent marker
- Ruler
- Bull's eye level (from hardware store)
- Small screws to mount level
- Graph paper
- Protractor
- Wood glue, or glue gun and hot glue

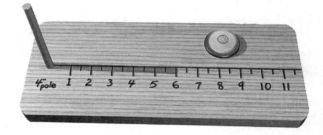

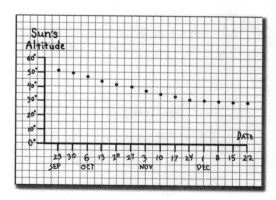

To Make the Shadow Tool

1. Cut a 14" long piece of the pine board.
2. Cut the dowel to a length of 4 and 5/8."
3. Draw a line down the middle of the board.
4. Drill a 3/8" diameter hole through the line about 1" from one end of the board. Make the hole perpendicular to the board. Glue the dowel in the hole with 4" on top.
5. Mark the line every half inch. Number each whole inch mark, starting at 1" from the base of the dowel.

To Use the Shadow Tool

1. At noon standard time face the shadow tool towards the sun. (Noon standard time is 1pm daylight savings time.)
2. Align the bubble in the level to make sure the shadow tool is level.
3. Record the length of the shadow.
4. Draw a triangle on graph paper. Use the shadow length as the triangle's base, and the dowel's height as the triangle's height. Draw the hypotenuse. Record the date and time.
5. Measure the angle between the base and the hypotenuse with a protractor. This is the sun's altitude.
6. Take shadow readings once a week from the Fall Equinox (September 23rd) until the Winter Solstice (December 22nd). Record the readings on graph paper to find the sun's altitude.
7. Make a graph of all the sun's altitudes from the Equinox to the Solstice.

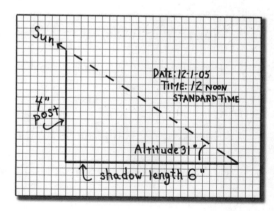

Some colors absorb light and heat better than others. Some colors are better at reflecting light and heat.

Guess which color gets the hottest, and test your guess by melting ice cubes on different colored surfaces.

Experiment with ways of making the ice cubes melt faster and slower.

Materials

- Construction paper of different colors
- Aluminum foil
- Same-sized ice cubes
- Cardboard (optional)
- Plastic wrap or plastic bags (optional)

What to Do

1. Guess which color will melt an ice cube fastest.

2. Put different colored pieces of paper (and a piece of aluminum foil) in the sun.

3. Place an ice cube on each surface.

4. See which ice cube melts first, and which melts last.

Which surface caused the ice cube to melt the fastest? Why?

OPTIONAL:

Put a piece of cardboard under the colored surfaces. Would this make any difference in how long it takes the ice cubes to melt? Why?

Now try putting the ice cubes in plastic bags, or covering them with plastic wrap. Would this make any difference in how long it takes the ice cubes to melt? Why?

Foam cups keep hot drinks hot, and cold drinks cold. That's because foam is a good insulator, and slows the movement of heat.

Your challenge is to use several kinds of insulation, and make a superinsulated cup. Then put an ice cube in the cup, and see how long the ice cube takes to melt.

It's even better to have a contest with several people, and see who does the best job of insulating. At the end of the contest, find out who's ice cube melts more slowly by measuring the amount of water in the cup.

Remember: the best insulation blocks radiation, convection and conduction!

Materials

- Paper or foam cups (with tops)
- Measuring cup or spoon (to measure water from cups)
- Masking Tape, Clear Tape, Glue (optional)
- Scissors
- Same-sized ice cubes
- INSULATION
    - Construction paper of different colors
    - Aluminum foil
    - Felt (or various fabrics)
    - Newspaper
    - Cardboard
    - Puffed cereal
    - Leaves or grass clippings
    - Packing materials: "peanuts", bubble wrap, etc.

What to Do

1. Each contestant insulates their cup to slow heat transfer. Try wrapping the cup with different things, like felt or bubble wrap. You can also make another container, and put the cup inside it. Then fill the outside container with insulation.

2. At a set time, everyone puts an ice cube in their cup, and places it in the sun.

3. After a certain amount of time has passed, remove the ice cubes from the cups.

4. Pour the water from each cup and measure it.

The contestant with the least amount of water wins!

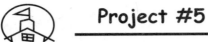

Have you noticed how a car parked in the sun stays warm inside, even on cold days? That's because clear materials like glass and plastic trap the heat from the sun. We can use this principle to make solar powered ovens.

Materials
- 1 Medium Sized Pizza Box
- Black Construction Paper
- Aluminum Foil
- 1 Reynolds Oven Cooking Bag (made of nylon that can take up to 400 degrees F.) You can get 8 windows out of each bag.
- Masking Tape, Clear Tape (about 1" wide), Glue (optional)
- Scissors (or Craft Knife if an adult helps)
- Pie Tins (or dark-colored oven-safe containers) to fit inside box
- Kabob stick (or wooden skewer) to hold flap open
- Newspaper for insulation
- Oven Thermometer (optional)

What to Do

1. Draw a line about 1" in from the edges of the box.

2. Cut along the line. *Don't cut along the top edge where the hinge of the box is!*

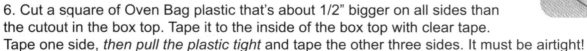

3. Gently fold the flap back along the uncut edge to form a crease.

4. Put a piece of aluminum foil on the inside of the flap, and fold the edges around the back of the flap. Have the shinier side facing up. Smooth the foil, and tape the edges on the back of the flap with masking tape. Keep the tape from showing on the front side of the flap. This foil will reflect sunlight into the box.

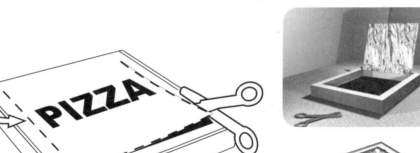

5. Open the box and put a piece of piece of cardboard in the bottom for more insulation. Cover it with black paper to help absorb the sun's energy.

6. Cut a square of Oven Bag plastic that's about 1/2" bigger on all sides than the cutout in the box top. Tape it to the inside of the box top with clear tape. Tape one side, *then pull the plastic tight* and tape the other three sides. It must be airtight!

7. Roll up some newspaper, and fit it around the inside edges of the box top. This is the insulation to hold the sun's heat. It should be 1" to 1.5" thick. Use tape to hold it in place.

8. Use the kabob stick to hold the top flap up. Adjust it to reflect as much sunlight as possible into the box. To hold it in place, stick it about an inch through the top, and tape the other end to the box

Have you noticed how a car parked in the sun stays warm inside, even on cold days? That's because clear materials like glass and plastic trap the heat from the sun. We can use this principle to make solar powered ovens.

Materials

- 1 Shoebox
- 1 Reynolds Oven Cooking Bag (made of nylon that can take up to 400 degrees F.) You can get 8 windows out of each bag.
- Aluminum Foil
- Black Construction Paper
- Masking Tape, Clear Tape (about 1" wide), Glue (optional)
- Scissors (or Craft Knife if an adult helps)
- Pie Tins (or dark-colored oven-safe containers) to fit inside box
- Kabob stick (or wooden skewer) to hold flap open
- Newspaper & cardboard for insulation
- Oven Thermometer (optional)

What to Do

1. Draw a line about 1" in from the edges of the box.

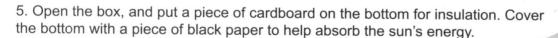

2. Cut along the line. *Don't cut along the top edge where the hinge of the box is!*

3. Gently fold the flap back along the uncut edge to form a crease.

4. Put a piece of aluminum foil on the inside of the flap, and fold the edges around the backside of the flap. Use the shinier side of the foil facing up, and try to smooth the foil. Tape the foil edges on the back of the flap with masking tape, keeping the tape from showing on the front side of the flap. This foil will reflect sunlight into the box.

5. Open the box, and put a piece of cardboard on the bottom for insulation. Cover the bottom with a piece of black paper to help absorb the sun's energy.

6. Make an inside wall of cardboard. You can do this by taping pieces together, or by cutting slots to join the pieces. Make sure the top of this wall is even with the outside wall of the box. Fill the space between the walls with rolled-up newspaper or other insulation. Make sure there are no gaps in the corners.

7. Cut a square of Oven Bag plastic that's about 1/2" bigger on all sides than the flap opening in the box top. Tape to the inside of the box top with clear tape. Tape one side, *then pull the plastic tight* and tape the other three sides. It must be airtight!

8. Make a thin roll of newspaper to use as a "gasket" between the box walls and the lid to retain heat.

Project #7 — Shoebox Solar Water Heater

The Shoebox Cooker in Project #6 can be used as a solar water heater too. Just put soda cans filled with water inside the cooker.

Materials

- 1 Shoebox Cooker (see Project #6)
- Oven Thermometer
- Soda Cans
- Black Paint (or wide tipped felt marker)
  OR
- Black Paper & Rubber Bands
- Extra kabob stick to hold flap open
- Aluminum Foil
- Masking Tape
- Scissors (or Craft Knife if an adult helps)
- Newspaper & carboard for insulation

What to Do

1. Paint a soda can black to absorb heat. If you don't have paint you can use a felt marker, or even wrap the can with black paper. Secure the paper with tape or rubber bands.

2. Use kabob stick to punch a hole through one of the long sides of the shoebox. The hole should be about 2" from the back of the box. This is for the thermometer.

3. You may want to add several layers of cardboard inside. This acts as insulation, and makes it easier for the thermometer to reach the can. Try wrapping the cardboard with aluminum foil to reflect heat onto the can.

4. (Optional) Attach another reflector with tape. Puncture the reflectors with kabob sticks, and and slide them through the reflectors. Use the sticks to hold the reflectors open.

5. Lay the shoebox on its side in the sun. You can lean it against a wall to face the sun. Fill the soda can about 3/4 full with water, and place it in the box. Insert the thermometer, and record the temperature. Take temperature readings at regular intervals (15 minutes or more). You can also record how long it takes the water to cool down after sunset.

6. (Optional) Try using a black-painted can and a plain can to see how fast each heats up. Make a chart to record your results.

Project #8

Shoebox Solar Home

Make a solar home model using an ordinary shoebox. Include solar features like south-facing windows with overhangs, thermal mass and photovoltaic cells.

Materials

- Shoebox & lid
- Masking tape, Clear tape, Glue sticks
- Scissors (or Craft Knife if an adult helps)
- Hot glue gun & glue sticks (optional)
- Pencil
- Ruler
- File folders for roof (legal size)
- Cardboard & construction paper
- Mini solar electric modules (optional)
- Fan motor & popsicle stick for blade (optional)
- Clear plastic for windows (packaging scraps work well)

What to Do

1. Cut a piece of cardboard to fit inside one end of the box.

2. Draw a line where the top of the box meets the cardboard.

3. Mark a point at the top of the cardboard, and make cuts from this mark to the ends of the line. This will be one side of the house.

4. Repeat these steps to make another side.

5. Tape or glue the sides inside the ends of the box.

6. Cut out the door. Be sure to cut only three sides so the door stays attached to the house. Fold it open.

7. Measure how wide and long the shoebox is. Multiply the length times the width to get the area of the floor.

   Example: 8" wide X 12" long = 96 square inches of floor area

8. To heat the house with sunlight, we'll have about 12 square inches of south-facing windows for every 100 square inches of floor area. This means we multiply the floor area by *0.12*

   Example: 96 X .12 = 11.5 or about 12 square inches of windows

9. A window 2' high and 3' long would be 6 square inches in area. Our example needs 2 windows this size. Calculate the windows you'll need, and cut them out. Be sure to cut only 3 sides so you can fold up the overhang. Put the windows on the long side of the shoebox.

10. Put the lid on the box, and use a file folder for the roof. You might have to trim the folder to fit.

11. Add other windows, plastic for glass, and other solar features. Draw tiles on construction paper for a thermal mass floor, or make a thermal mass wall. You can even put solar cells on the roof, and power a small fan or lights.

Project #9   Custom Solar Home Model

Design and build a model solar home the way architects do: using plans drawn to scale. This project guide shows a sample solar home: the saltbox house.

Materials
- Ruler or Architect's scale (optional)
- Hot glue gun and glue sticks, &/or glue
- Scissors (or Craft Knife if an adult helps)
- Pencil
- Right triangle
- Cardboard
- Mini solar electric modules (optional)
- Fan motor & popsicle stick for blade (optional)
- Graph paper: 4 squares per inch is recommended

Objective
Make a model home that uses sunlight to heat the building, heat water and make electricity. Design the home to stay cooler in the summer too. Use the solar design principles from Chapter 5:
1. South-facing windows and glass doors to catch the winter sun's energy.
2. Insulation to keep heat in during the winter, and keep heat out in the summer.
3. Thermal mass to store heat in the winter, and store "coolth" in the summer.
4. Overhangs to block the summer sun.
5. Air circulation: ventilation and convection currents to stay cooler in the summer.

Making Plans
Start by drawing 3 or 4 views of the home. The first view is the Plan View, or floorplan. It's what you'd see looking down on the model with the roof off. The views are drawn to scale on graph paper. Each square on the paper represents a certain number of feet in the actual home. We'll use a scale of 1 square (1/4 inch) equals 1 foot.

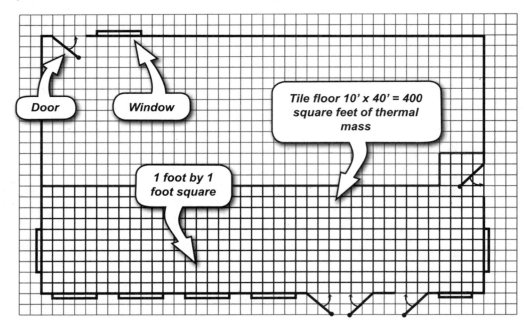

PLAN VIEW

**40 feet long
24 feet wide**

South

Door

Window

Tile floor 10' x 40' = 400 square feet of thermal mass

1 foot by 1 foot square

Total area of first floor: 24' x 40' = 960 square feet

Calculating the Amount of South Facing Glass

Each window facing south is a solar heating machine. The amount of south facing glass depends on many things, including: where the home is, how well it's insulated, and how much sunlight is available year round. To estimate how much south glass we need, we'll aim for 12 square feet of glass for every 100 square feet of floor area. This means we multiply the floor area by **0.12**.

1st find the AREA of floor space (first floor), by multiplying the length of the home by the width:

40 feet x 24 feet = 960 square feet of area on the first floor

Then use this area to find out how much south facing glass to put in the first floor of the house:

960 sq. ft. x 0.12 = 115 sq. ft. of south facing glass on the first floor

This doesn't need to be exact. 100 sq. ft. of south facing glass would still do a good job of heating the house. 60 sq. ft. isn't as good, but it's much better than nothing.

South Elevation

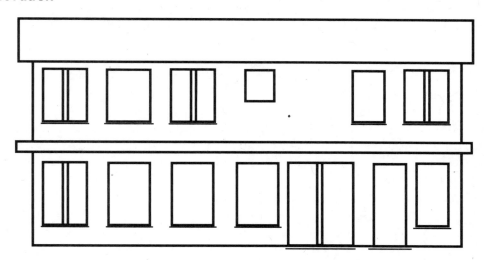

The south elevation shows what the south side of the house looks like. We'll sketch in enough windows to fully heat the house. On the first floor we've put 4 windows of 16 sq. ft each, 3 glass door sections with 12 sq. ft. of glass each, and a narrow window with 12 sq. ft. of glass.

4 windows x 16 sq. ft. = 64 sq. ft.; 3 doors x 12 sq. ft. = 36; 1 window x 12 sq. ft. = 12

Add the products up:

64 sq. ft. + 36 sq. ft. + 12 sq. ft. = 112 sq. ft.

We're happy; this amount is very close to our goal of 115 square feet of south facing glass. We should repeat these steps to calculate the solar gain (south-facing glass) for the 2nd floor.

Thermal Mass

There needs to be enough thermal mass in the house to absorb the sunlight coming through the windows. If there isn't, the house will overheat. It's best if the thermal mass is uncovered, and the sun shines directly on it.

Calculating the Amount of Thermal Mass

The area of thermal mass depends on many things too. A thermal mass area that's at least 3 times the south glass area is a good place to start. Having extra thermal mass is fine. This means we multiply the south glass area by 3:

112 sq. ft. of south glass x 3 = 336 sq. ft. of thermal mas needed on the first floor

We have enough thermal mass with the tile floor on the south side of the house:

10 ft. x 40 ft. = 400 sq. ft. of thermal mass (tile floor)

Repeat these steps to find the thermal mass needed for the 2nd floor.

East Elevation

The east elevation shows the roof overhangs (eaves) so we can be sure the sun shines in during the winter, but not during the summer. To see how big an overhang we need, we have to know how high the sun will get in the summer, and how low it will be in the winter. The sun's height is an angle called the sun's *altitude*, and it depends on our latitude.

You can find the sun's highest altitude on any day of the year at the U.S. Naval Observatory website. Enter your city and the date, then find the highest altitude around 12 noon on that day:

http://aa.usno.navy.mil/data/docs/AltAz.html

You can also figure out the sun's highest and lowest altitude with these equations:

Sun's altitude at noon on summer solstice = 90 + 23.5 - (your latitude)
Sun's altitude at noon on winter solstice = 90 - 23.5 - (your latitude)

To find the latitude for your city, & a link to the U.S. Naval Observatory website, visit: *www.solarschoolhouse.org*

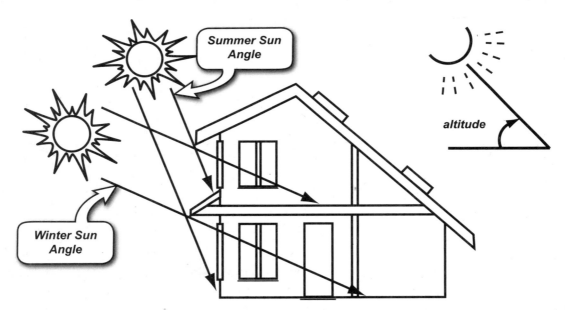

East Elevation showing the sun's highest altitude at the winter and summer solstices

The East Elevation (above) shows us that the winter sun will shine deeply into the building, and heat the tile floor directly. The overhangs will block the summer sun.

Calculating Overhangs

Example: Our sample saltbox house is at San Francisco, about 38.5 degrees north latitude. To find the sun's highest altitude in the summer:

90 + 23.5 - (38.5) = 75 degrees

Use a protractor and ruler to see how big the overhangs need to be. Align the ruler at 75 degrees, and make sure the ruler touches the bottom of the window.

Draw a line along the ruler. The overhang has to touch this line to shade the window on the summer solstice.

Use 90 - 23.5 - 38.5 to find the winter sun angle.

North Elevation

The main purpose of the North Elevation is to plan the minimal window space on the north side of the house. This is to reduce the energy lost through the glass. One still wants windows for bringing light into the building and for cross-ventilation. Having a drawing of the north side of the building is also helpful for building our models.

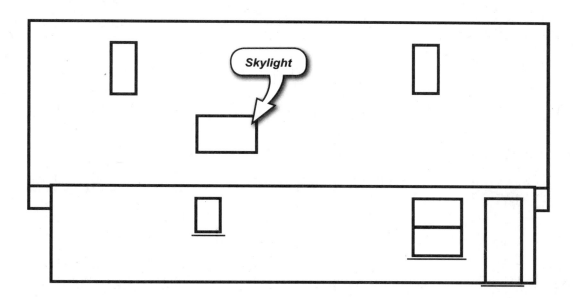

Note also the placement of three skylights for daylighting on the north roof. Skylights do cause some heat loss. Avoid skylights on the south facing roof as they may cause the house to over heat in the summer. Openable skylights are useful in warm months for venting off extra heat.

Note: The numbers for window area and mass area are general guidelines. Climates with hot summers and mild winters could use less window area; climates with mild summers and cold winters would need more south glass area and more thermal mass.

Project #10   Read Your Electric Meter

It's easy to read your electric meter if you understand some basic rules. Each small dial represents one digit of the present reading. These dials turn both clockwise and counter clockwise. When a hand is between numbers, record the smaller number.

If you can't tell if a hand is past a number or not, just look at the dial to the right. If it has passed zero, then the hand is pointing to the correct number. If the dial to the right has not passed zero, then use the next smaller number.

Let's try an example:

Reading on Monday

| 4 | 6 | 3 | 9 | 2 |

10 thousands   thousands   hundreds   tens   ones

The third digit is a three because the hand to the right has not yet passed zero. If the second dial from the right was between the zero and the one, then the third digit would have been a four.

Now figure out the next day's reading:

Reading on Tuesday

| 4 | 6 | | | |

10 thousands   thousands   hundreds   tens   ones

Once you determine Tuesday's reading, subtract Monday's reading from it to find out how much energy (kilowatt hours) was used in the day between the 2 readings.

Tuesday: 46, _____ kWh
Monday: - 4 6 , 3 9 2 kWh
Energy used = _____ kWh

Try recording readings at your home for several days in a row. By subtracting yesterday's reading from today's reading, you can get a feel for how much energy (kilowatt hours) you use each day.

Instant Electric "DEMAND" Reading from a Electric Meter

To find out how fast you're using electricity right now:

1. Note Kh found on the meter face (A).
2. Select a number of revolutions to be counted (B)
3. Time how long the revolutions take in seconds (C)
5. Apply the following formula:

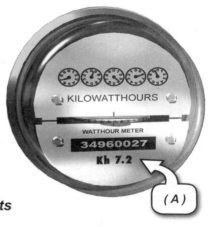

(A)

$$Demand = Kilowatt\ [kW] = \frac{3.6 \times A \times B}{C}$$

Example: A = 7.2 Kh, B = 1, C = 30 seconds

$$Demand = Kilowatt\ [kW] = \frac{3.6 \times 7.2 \times 1}{30} = .864\ kW = 864\ watts$$

If this meter is on a PV array, this is the amount of Power that is being produced by the PV array at this instant. This value will change throughout the day based on the available sunlight.

Find out how much energy and money you can save by using energy efficient lighting. Pick a room in your house that is used a lot. Then pick the regular (incandescent) light bulb in the room that is used the most. Do the following steps; use a calculator if you like:

Step 1: Find out how much it costs to power the light.

_____ watts (write in bulb wattage)

x_____ # of hours a day the light is on (round to closest full hour)

=_____ total energy used in one day. (This is called watt-hours)

x 30 (average # of days in each month)

=_____ energy used in a month (in watt-hours)

÷ by 1000 to convert watt-hours to kilowatt-hours or KWH (this is what you see on your electric bill)

=_____ approximate KWH per month

x $0.15 ($0.15 per KWH is about what you're charged for electricity)

= $_____ this is about how much you pay each month to power the light.

Step 2: Pick a replacement fluorescent light bulb that uses less energy (watts), but gives the same amount of light.

Regular Lightbulb	Compact Fluorescent	Amount of Light
60 watts	15 watts	900 lumens
75 watts	18 watts	1200 lumens
100 watts	23 watts	1500 lumens
120 watts	30 watts	1800 lumens

Step 1: Find out how much it costs to power the new fluorescent light.

_____ watts (new bulb wattage)

x_____ # of hours used per day (same hours you used before)

=_____ watt-hours per day

x 30 (average # of days in each month)

=_____ watt-hours per month

÷ by 1000 to convert to KWH

=_____ approximate KWH per month

x $0.15 per KWH

= $_____ this is about how much you pay each month to power the new light.

Step 4: Subtract to see how much you save each month by changing the bulb.

$_____ cost per month of old light

- $_____ cost per month of new light

$_____ monthly savings

Step 4: Subtract to see how much energy you can save by changing the bulb.

_____ KWH per month (old light)

- _____ KWH per month (new light)

_____ KWH per month saved

x 12 _____ KWH per year saved

x 5 _____ KWH saved per year by replacing the 5 most-used lightbulbs in the house.

Project designed by Andrea Long

Project #12   Series and Parallel Circuits

Wire solar cells to a small DC motor. Watch what happens with series and parallel circuits. Find out how to make the motor turn faster, and which circuit works better on a cloudy day.

Materials
- Solar cells
- Direct current hobby motor
- Plastic wheel (optional)
- Jumpers with alligator clip ends

NOTE: This project uses the Solar Cell Classroom Set from the Solar Schoolhouse (www.solarschoolhouse.org). These circuits can be made with other small solar cells and loads.

Simple Circuit to Motor

1. Use jumpers to connect wires from the solar cell to the terminals on the motor. Notice which way the motor spins. The plastic wheel makes it easier to see which way the motor is turning.

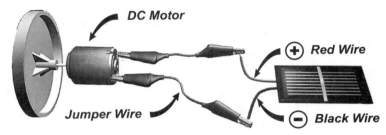

2. Reverse polarity by switching the jumpers on the motor terminals, and observe. *What happens when you reverse polarity?*

Series Circuit to Motor

1. Use a jumper to connect the black (-) wire of one cell to the red (+) wire of another cell.
2. Use jumpers to connect the remaining wire from each cell to the terminals on the motor. What happens?
3. Connect more cells in series, and notice motor speed.

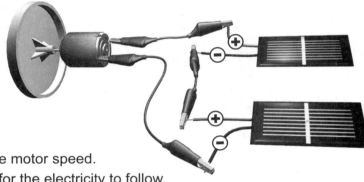

NOTE: Series circuits have only one path for the electricity to follow.
What happens when you shade one cell? Why do you think this happens in a series circuit?

Parallel Circuit to Motor

1. Use one end of a jumper to clamp the red wires from two solar cells together, and clip the other end to a terminal on the motor.
2. Use a jumper to clamp the black wires from the two solar cells together, and clip the other end to the other terminal on the motor.

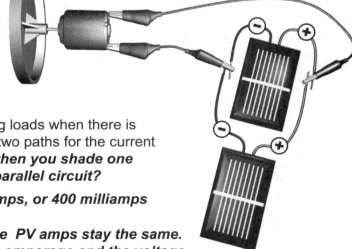

NOTE: Parallel circuits are useful for powering loads when there is less sunlight, like on a cloudy day. There are two paths for the current to follow between the cells. *What happens when you shade one cell? Why do you think this happens in a parallel circuit?*

Each solar cell produces .5 volts and .4 Amps, or 400 milliamps (mA) in maximum sun.
Series wiring (+ t o -) adds the voltage. The PV amps stay the same.
Parallel wiring (- t o - and + to +) adds the amperage and the voltage stays the same.

Imagine the power is out at your house and you want to listen to the radio. You're in luck! You have six solar cells, and it's a sunny day. All you need to do is figure out how to connect them to the radio.

You know the following information:

1. Each solar cell produces .5 volts and 0.4 amps in full sun.

2. The radio needs 3 volts and 0.3 amps.

Draw the wires between the solar cells, and connect them to the radio wires.

Remember:
Wiring cells in series (+ to -, + to -) adds volts, PV amps stay the same.
Wiring cells in parallel (+ to +, - to -) adds amps, volts stay the same.

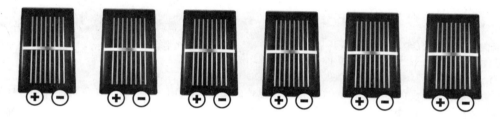

Final output of solar cells:

_____ *volts*

_____ *amps*

What kind of wiring method did you use? _____

How much power (in watts) does the radio use? _____

Power formula: watts = volts x amps

Project #14   Solar Race Car Model

Make a solar powered model car and have races! Learn about gear ratios, reducing friction, and how to make model cars that are lightweight and strong. This sample car uses a kit of wheels, motor and gears. The car body is made of wood, but all kinds of materials can be used including: foamboard, cardboard, plastic containers, parts from broken VCRs, etc. Cars have even been made from CDs and plastic soda bottles. Use your imagination! These are just guidelines.

NOTE: This project uses knives and hot glue, and should be done with the help of an adult!

Equipment Suppliers:

Solar World: *www.solar-world.com* (719) 635-5125 has:
- Axle gears, wheels, axles (Jr. Solar Sprint Accessory Bag JSS-ACC)
- DC mounting brackets and motor gears (Jr.Solar Sprint JSS-B/G)
- 3 watt modules (3 volt x 1 amp) Shell Solar Modules
- DC motors (solar world JSS-M)

**Pitsco: *www.shop-pitsco.com* ** has:
- lightweight modules ("Ray Catcher")
- various gears and wheels

From local craft and hobby stores:

- small screweyes (for axles and car guides)
- velcro or rubber bands for attaching solar module to car
- 3/16" by 3/16" by 24" lenghts of basswood (about 4 - 5 per car body)
- 1/8" by 4" by 24' lengths of basswood for motor base (about 3" x 4" per car, use 1 sheet for 7 cars)
- jumper wires with alligator clip ends to connect the motor to the module
- Fishing line for track guideline (30 to 60 lb. test)

Tools:

- Side cutters to cut basswood sticks
- Hot glue gun and glue sticks
- Tiny phillips screwdriver
- Wire cutter and stripper
- Small pliers
- Drill and 1/16" drill bits
- Small hobby saws and utility kinves

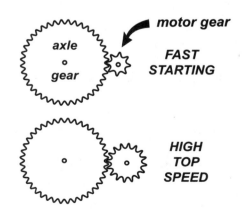

The motor can go on the top or bottom of the frame.

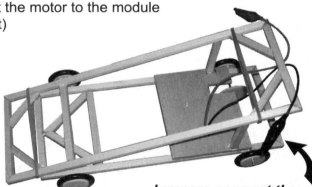

Jumpers connect the motor to the solar module.

Gearing

1. Decide which gears to use. The biggest gear goes on the axle. One of the smaller gears goes on the motor.

The more teeth the *motor gear* has, the faster the car will go, and the longer it will take to reach that speed. If you use the smallest gear on the motor, the car will accelerate quickly, but not reach as high a speed.

2. Slide the big gear onto the axle, holding the axle with pliers. Be careful not to bend the axle. If the gear is too tight to slide, drill the hole bigger with the 1/16" bit. If you drill the hole too big, and the gear slips on the axle, use hot glue in the hole.

axle gear · *motor gear* · **FAST STARTING**

HIGH TOP SPEED

Mounting the Motor

1. Measure the width of the solar module. Cut a piece of the 4" basswood to be as long as the module is wide. Cut a notch to make room for the axle gear.
2. Put the motor bracket on the basswood, and mark the points where screws will go with a pencil. Drill 1/16" starter holes through the pencil marks.
3. Put the motor into the bracket, and slide the gear onto the motor shaft. Lock the motor with the set-screw, and screw the bracket to the basswood.

Making the Frame

1. Use the 3/16" sticks to make a box as wide as the solar module, and a little bit longer. Hot glue the joints, making sure the box is square.
2. Put the motor mount on the frame to mark its position. Remove the mount.
3. The axles will be held on with screw eyes. Mark points for the screw eye holes on the front and back of the frame. Keep the axles square with the frame so the car will drive straight (or be sure the axles are parallel to each other).
4. Drill 1/16" starter holes at the pencil marks, and screw in the screw eyes.
5 Put a wheel on an axle, slip the axle through a screweye, and slide on the big gear. Slip the axle through the other screw eye. Slide the wheels close to the screw eyes, or the gears may slip out of position.

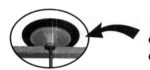

Keep the wheels close to the screweyes or the gears may slip out of place. Leave enough room for the wheels to spin freely.

Attaching the Motor Mount

Be sure the gears fit firmly.

1. Put the motor mount on the frame, and make sure the gears line up snugly. Screw the mount to the frame.

Mounting the Solar Module

1. Use the 3/16" sticks to build a framework for the solar module. Try to make it both light and strong. It can be titled to a certain sun angle, or kept low to cut wind resistance. Remember to put a bumper in front to hold and protect the module.
2. Screw a screweye into the bottom of the frame at each end. These will hold the car to a fishing line guide on the racetrack. Before attaching the screweyes, open them a little with pliers so you'll be able to slip the fishing line through.
3. Attach the module with big rubber bands, or glue velcro to the module and the frame.
4. Clip jumper wires from the motor terminals to the module leads. The clips can act as a switch.

Screw eyes hold the car to fishing line on the track.

Racing

1. For a track use a flat smooth surface, like a tennis court. Have two people for each car: one to release the car, and one to catch it.
2. Tie thick fishing line to heavy weights at each end of the track (cinder blocks work well). The line should be 1" to 3" above the ground. Slip the fishing line into the car's screweyes.
3. To start the race: racers lift the cardboard shading the solar panel on each car.

NOTE: This project uses the Solar Technology Kit available from the Solar Schoolhouse. (www.solarschoolhouse.org)

Build and test several solar electric circuits with the Solar Power Monitor! Practice wiring solar modules in series and parallel to change voltage and amperage. Experiment with the photovoltaic effect by wiring modules in short circuit and changing module angles to the Sun.

Build circuits to power various DC loads, including a water pump.

CAUTION: For use only with DC power! Fan and light need 12-20 volts DC. Voltage for output loads will vary.

The Solar Power Monitor is a plexiglas circuit board with ports for plugging in solar modules. It also has meters to measure current and voltage. There are two small DC loads (a light and fan) on the Monitor, places to connect external loads, and switches to turn loads on and off.

Other items included with the Solar Power Monitor:

- Compass - to see which direction produces the most power.
- Protractor & Ruler - for studying Sun Angles (Solar Geometry)
- Jumpers with alligator clip ends - set of 10. To connect modules in series, and short circuit switch #3 when testing solar modules.
- Test Leads (Red & Black) - 3 sets. With banana plug on one end and alligator clip on the other. For connecting modules to the Power Monitor, or to connect external loads (such as the water pump) to the power monitor.
- 3 Watt Solar Modules - 8 frameless silicon crystal PV modules. 3 volts, 1.2 amps DC each
- 12 volt DC Water pump

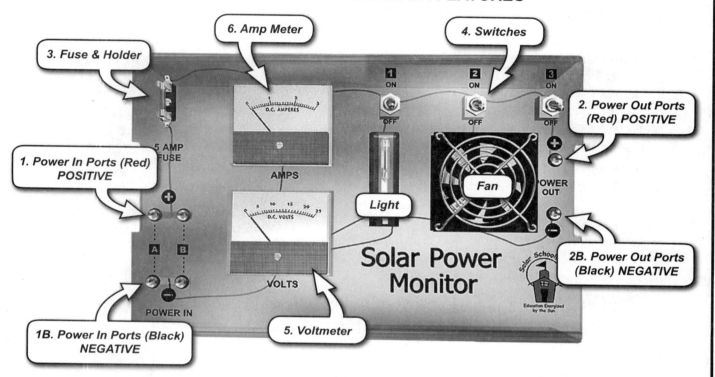

SOLAR POWER MONITOR FEATURES

6. Amp Meter

4. Switches

3. Fuse & Holder

2. Power Out Ports (Red) POSITIVE

1. Power In Ports (Red) POSITIVE

2B. Power Out Ports (Black) NEGATIVE

1B. Power In Ports (Black) NEGATIVE

5. Voltmeter

1. **POWER INPUT PORTS:** For inserting leads to connect Solar Modules. *NOTE:* There are two pairs of Input Ports (red and black make a pair). Connect one module to each pair for *parallel wiring*.

2. **POWER OUTPUT PORTS:** For inserting leads to power external loads, like the water pump. *NOTE:* Switch #3 must be turned on to power external loads.

3. **FUSE:** Wired in the positive side of the circuit, it acts as overcurrent protection. For example, if a battery is connected to the Power In Ports, and a jumper short circuits the Power Out Ports (or a load connected to the Power Out Ports is short circuited), the battery will dump too much energy all at once, and damage the Power Monitor. To prevent this, the fuse melts, breaks the circuit, and protects the Power Monitor.

4. **SWITCHES:** Wired in parallel to separately control the Light (#1), Fan (#2), & Ext. Load (#3).

5. **VOLTMETER:** Measures voltage, and shows if you have enough for a specific load. For example, if you wire three of the 3-volt modules in series to power a 9 volt radio, the voltmeter will show about 9 volts. If polarity is reversed (+ and - wires in the wrong ports), the needle will go below the "0" mark. This helps prevent wiring a radio backwards, which can damage the radio. Polarity determines the direction in which the electricity flows.

6. **AMP METER:** Measures the electric current flowing through the circuit. For amps to show on the meter a switch must be turned on, and connected to a load. It's okay to short circuit solar modules by connecting the Power Out Ports with a jumper. This shows the maximum amps the module can provide. Different loads need different amounts of current. The light on switch #1 glows at 0.1 Amps and is bright at 0.3 Amps. The fan runs strong at 0.1 Amps.

MEASURING MODULE OUTPUT

One of the 1st things you can do with the Power Monitor is check the maximum voltage and current your solar modules can supply.

The modules are rated at 3 volts, but this varies with load and sunlight. In test conditions, the modules will produce more than 3 volts of electrical pressure. Here's how:

Measure the Maximum Voltage

1. Plug leads (banana plug ends) into one positive and one negative Input Port. Clip the other ends to the module wires. Red = ⊕, black = ⊖

2. Record the Voltmeter reading with all switches off. This is the **open circuit voltage** (Voc), the maximum module voltage when no current is flowing. If the reading is below 0, reverse the alligator clips connected to the solar module.

3. Check the Amp Meter. What does it read? Why?

Measuring Maximum Voltage

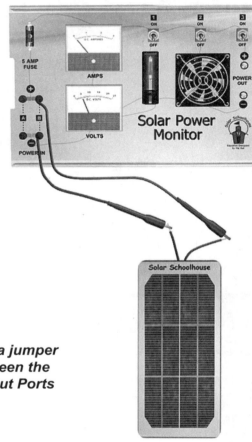

Measuring Maximum Amperage

Clip a jumper between the Output Ports

Measure the Maximum Amperage (Current)

1. Clip a jumper between the Output Ports. Turn on switch #3.

2. Record the Amp Meter reading. This is the **short-circuit current** (Isc), the maximum current possible without a load. Normal loads will draw less current.

3. Experiment with the current produced by changing the module's angle to the Sun.

4. Check the voltmeter. What does it read? Why?

MAKING A SERIES STRING - Series Wiring

A **series string** is any number of photovoltaic modules connected **in series** to give a single electrical output. Let's wire four solar modules in series to make a series string. Remember:

SERIES WIRING (⊕ to ⊖) ADDS VOLTS.

Connect Four 3 Volt Modules to Make a 12 Volt Series String

1. Connect the positive wire (red) of each module to the negative wire (black) of the next with jumpers.

2. Connect the end wires of the group of modules to the Power Monitor Input Ports with test leads.

TIP: Tie an overhand knot to shorten the jumpers.

The Voltmeter should read above 12 volts in full sun with no load.

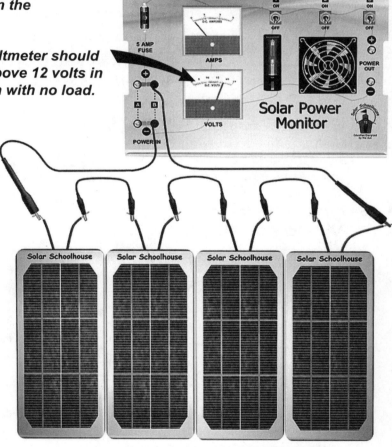

3. Check the Voltmeter. With the switches off, the **open circuit voltage** should be above 12 volts.

If the reading is below 0, the polarity is reversed. Switch the series string test lead clips to correct this.

If there is no voltage, part of your circuit isn't connected. Check connections.

Measure the Load Amperage

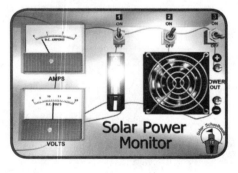

Four 3 Volt Modules in a 12 Volt Series String

1. Turn on switch #1 to power the light. Check the Amp Meter reading. This is the current drawn by the light. Remember: the light and fan need 12 volts to operate.

2. Turn on switch #2, and check the Amp Meter. This is the total current drawn by both loads.

3. Try attaching the water pump (see next page). Be sure to submerge the pump in water before turning on switch #3. The pump should work, but not at full power. To increase the power of the pump, connect another series string in parallel (see next page).

MAKING A SOLAR ARRAY - Series/Parallel Wiring

To run at full power, the water pump needs more current than one series string provides. We want to increase the current, but not the voltage. We can wire a second series string to the Power Monitor *in parallel*. This is called *series/parallel* wiring. Remember:

PARALLEL WIRING (⊕ to ⊕, ⊖ to ⊖) ADDS PV AMPS.

The entire group of solar modules is called a *solar array*. A solar array is any number of photovoltaic modules connected together to provide a single electrical output.

Make a Solar Array with Two Series Strings.

1. Make a 2nd four module series string (see last page).

2. Connect the end wires of the 2nd string to the 2nd set of Input Ports on the Power Monitor.

3. Check the open circuit voltage with switch #3 off. It should be the same as one series string.

4. With the pump in water, turn on switch #3, and check the Amp Meter. It should read higher than it did for one string, and the pump should work very well.

Connect series strings in parallel: positive to positive (red to red), and negative to negative (black to black).

Be sure all modules are aimed at full sun, and not shaded.

PUT THE PUMP IN WATER BEFORE TURNING ON SWITCH #3.

The Voltmeter will read the same with 2 series strings; the Amp Meter will increase.

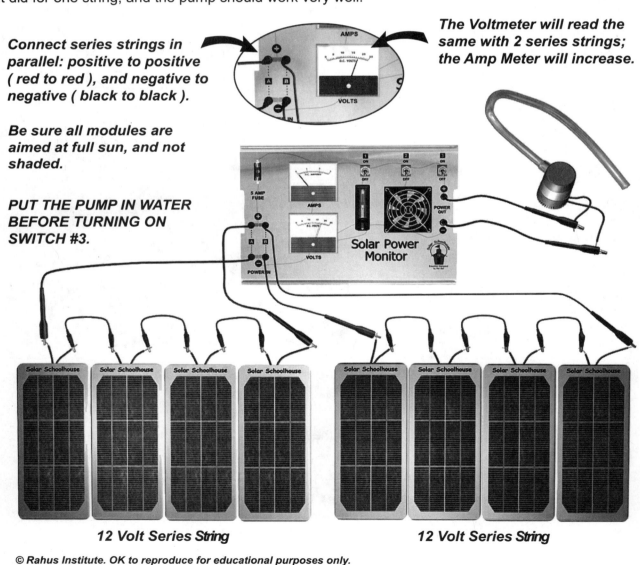

12 Volt Series String   *12 Volt Series String*

Glossary

A

AC electricity Electric current that changes direction many times per second.

alternating current See *AC electricity*.

ampere The unit of electrical current, often abreviated as "amp". A number of electrical charges flowing past a point in one second.

Autumnal Equinox The beginning of autumn. Around September 23rd in the Northern Hemisphere. Day and night are the same length.

B

battery backup system A solar electric system using batteries to store photovoltaic electricity.

breadbox heater Simple solar water heater using a tank of water in a glass-covered insulated box aimed at the sun.

C

circuit breakers An automatic switch that stops the flow of electric current in an overloaded electric circuit.

compact fluorescent lamps An energy saving lightbulb with an integrated ballast.

conduction 1. The way heat moves through a solid by vibration of particles (atoms, molecules). 2. The way an electric current is carried through substances by the movement of free electrons.

conductors 1. A substance through which heat can easily flow. 2. A substance through which electric current can flow.

convection The way heat moves through fluids (liquids and gases). The area closest to the heat source expands and rises. The cooler area sinks.

convection current Movement of fluids by convection

D

Daylighting Use of indirect sunlight to light building interiors and reduce electrical demand.

DC electricity Electric current that moves in only one direction.

deciduous trees Trees that lose their leaves in the fall.

direct current See *DC electricity*.

direct gain Solar design that uses sun-facing windows to allow sunlight to heat thermal mass.

drainback system Solar hot water system using two separate tanks connected by a heat exchanger. The fluid in the solar collector drains back into one tank when tempertures fall.

E

electrical circuit The path through which an electric current flows.

electrical current The flow of electrically charged particles. Measured in amperes.

electrical insulator A susbtance that resists the flow of electrical current.

electric meter Device for measuring electricity consumption

electromagnetic waves Radiation consisting of waves of energy, including radio waves, infrared, visible light, ultraviolet, X rays, and gamma rays.

electrons Negatively charged particles existing around the nucleui of atoms.

energy audit An evaluation of the way energy is used.

energy efficiency The ability to perform work using the least amount of energy.

Energy Guide Label Label attached to new appliances estimating projected energy use in comparison with similar models.

equator An imaginary circle around the middle of the Earth separating the north and south hemispheres.

evergreen trees Trees that keep their leaves throughout the year.

F

flat plate solar collector A device that transfers the sun's heat to a fluid using tubes attached to a dark-colored sheet.

full sun equivalent See *Peak Sun*.

fuse Safety device containing a metal element that melts, and opens the circuit, when current exceeds a specific amperage.

G

greenhouse effect A warming that happens when solar radiation is trapped by a substance which lets sunshine pass through, but absorbs radiated heat. This substance can be the glass in a greenhouse, or gases in the atmosphere.

H

heat exchanger A device that transfers heat from a fluid on one side of a barrier to a fluid on the other side without bringing the fluids into direct contact.

hemisphere One half of a sphere separated by a great circle, such as the Northern Hemisphere of the Earth.

hours of use The total number of hours an electrical device draws current over a given period of time.

I

indirect sunlight Sunlight that has been reflected or diffused. See Daylighting

infiltration Air leaking into a building through cracks and spaces, especially around doors and windows.

infrared radiation Also called heat. Electromagnetic radiation with wavelengths longer than visible light and shorter than radio waves. Given off by anything hot.

insulators 1. Substances that do not conduct electricity. 2. Substances that do not conduct heat well.

inverter Electrical device that changes DC electricity into AC electricity. Special inverters can synchronize with the utilty grid, and allow PV power to backfeed into the grid.

isolated gain systems A solar design in which sunlight is collected in an area that can be closed off from the rest of the house.

K

kilowatt (kW) A rate of energy used or produced (power) equal to 1,000 watts.

kilowatt-hour (kWh) An amount of energy used or produced, equal to 1 killowatt for 1 hour.

L

latitude The angular distance north or south of the earth's equator, measured in degrees along a meridian.

load Any device using energy (electricity).

low-e glass Glass coated with a material (usually metal) to reduce the movement of heat.

light shelf A horizontal overhang between two windows to shade the lower window, and reflect light through the upper window..

M

Magnetic Declination The angular difference between the true north pole and the magnetic north pole.

N

net metering A method of accounting in which electricity sold to the utility by their customer is given full retail credit.

nucleus The center of an atom containing protons and (except hydrogen) nuetrons.

O

overhangs Horizontal projections on buildings that shade windows.

P

parallel wiring An electrical circuit with more than one path for current to follow. Made by connecting plus to plus and minus to minus. Increases current without affecting voltage.

passive solar design Using the sun to heat and cool buildings, with little or no use of machines or other fuel.

peak sun The maximum solar energy received at any one instant, anywhere on Earth. Equal to 1 killowatt per square meter.

peak sun hours The amount of radiant energy equal to one hour of peak sun. 1 peak sun hour equals 1 kilowatt hour per square meter.

peak sun hours per day The total amount of radiant energy received per day.

phantom loads Loads that consume energy even when turned "off".

photons Individual "packets" of light or electromagnetic radiation.

photovoltaic array A number of photovoltaic modules connected together.

photovoltaic cell A single semiconductor that converts light into electricity.

photovoltaic effect The basic physical process through which a solar cell produces voltage when exposed to radiant energy (especially light).

photovoltaic modules A group of PV cells connected together, and sealed for protection from the environment.

protons A positively charged subatomic particle in the nucleus of an atom.

PV direct system An electrical device connected directly to a photovoltaic supply.

R

radiation Energy radiated or transmitted as rays, waves, or in the form of particles (photons). The most efficient form of heat transfer, requiring no material to conduct heat.

rate of energy use A measurement of the speed at which energy is used. Also called "power". See *Watt*.

S

series wiring An electric circuit in which the current passes through one element after another, following only one path. Made by connecting plus to minus and plus to minus. Increases voltage without affecting current.

solar array See *Photovoltaic Array*.

solar collector Common term for solar water heating panel used to "collect" the sun's heat and transfer it to a fluid.

solar panels Common term for a panel which converts light imto electricity. See *Photovoltaic Module*.

Summer Solstice The time of year when the sun's arc is highest in the sky. On or about June 21 in the Northern Hemisphere.

sunspace A separate, glassed in room used to accept and store solar heat for transfer to the main building.

suntempering The simplest passive solar design using sun-facing windows to accept solar heat.

T

tankless water heater A device using a heat exchanger to rapidly heat water flowing through it. Also called a demand water heater.

thermal mass Material used to absorb and store heat. Reduces temperature swings, and allows for later use of stored heat.

thermosiphon system A solar water heating system that doesn't need pumps. The collector is below the storage tank, and the rising hot water causes circulation.

Trombe walls a sun-facing thermal mass wall built combined with an air space to form a large solar thermal collector. The wall is named after the inventor Felix Trombe, who popularized the design in 1964. Edward Morse patented the design in 1881.

U

utility grid The transmission and distribution system supping electricity to homes and businesses. Also called the Electrical Grid.

utility intertie system A solar electric system using a special inverter that can pump electricity from the solar panels into the utility grid.

V

valance A horizontal structure on the inside of a window often supporting curtains. Reduces heat loss from windows.

vampires Inefficient transformers for small appliances which are always "on" and wasting energy.

Vernal Equinox The beginning of spring. Around March 21 in the Northern Hemisphere, Day and night are the same length.

voltage The pressure "pushing" electrons in an electric circuit.

volt A measure of electrical "pressure", or force.

W

watt A unit of power. A measure of the speed at which electrical energy is used or produced. Named after James Watt, a british engineer who improved the steam engine.

watt-hour An amount of energy used or produced equal to 1 watt for 1 hour.

wattage Rate of energy flow, often used to describe the electrical requirement of an appliance or load.

Winter Solstice The time of year when the sun's arc is lowest in the sky. On or about december 22 in the Northern Hemisphere.

Index

A

AC electricity 73
alternating current 73
ampere 69
Autumnal Equinox 13

B

battery backup system 72
blinds 55
breadbox heater 36

C

circuit breakers 68
clerestory windows 56
compact fluorescent lamps 85
conduction 23
conductors of electricity 68
conductors of heat 23
convection current 23
curtains 55

D

DC electricity 73
deciduous 48
direct current 73
direct gain 51
drainback system 39

E

electrical circuit 68
electrical current 65
electrical insulator 68
electric bill 91
electric meter 73, 92
electromagnetic waves 21
electrons 65
energy audit 88
energy efficiency 84
energy guide label 87
equator 12
evergreens 48

F

flat plate solar collector 37
full sun equivalent 94
fuses 68

G

greenhouse effect 30
gridtie system 74

H

heat exchanger 40
hemispheres 12
hours of use 91

I

infiltration 50
infrared radiation 21
insulators 24
inverter 74
isolated gain systems 51

K

kilowatt 88
kilowatt-hour 89

L

latitude 67
light shelf 55
load 68
low-e glass 49

M

module output 95

N

net metering 74
nucleus 65

O

overhangs 54

P

parallel wiring 71
peak sun 94
peak sun hours 94
peak sun hours per day 95
phantom loads 87
photons 21, 64
photovoltaic array 66
photovoltaic cell 64
photovoltaic effect 65
photovoltaic modules 66

power formula 71
power used by appliances 90
protons 65
PV direct system 72

R

radiation 21
rate of energy use 88
referigerators 86

S

series wiring 70
skylights 55
solar array 66
solar collector 37
solar greenhouse 51
solar panels 66
Summer Solstice 13
sunspace 51
suntempering 49
system sizing worksheet 96

T

tankless water heater 40
thermal mass 50
thermosiphon system 38
Trombe walls 52

U

utility grid 73
utility intertie system 74

V

valance 55
vampires 87
Vernal Equinox 13
voltage 69
voltage source 68
volts 68

W

water heater 36
watt 69, 88
watt-hour 89
wattage 89
Winter Solstice 13